GREAT LIVES

Lord Byron

GREAT LIVES

Lord Byron

Peter Brent

Introduction by Elizabeth Longford

Book Club Associates London

House editor Enid Gordon
Art editor Andrew Shoolbred
Picture research Colleen Chesterman
Layout by Juanita Grout

Filmset and printed in Great Britain by
Cox & Wyman Ltd, London, Fakenham and Reading

Contents

Introduction

BYRON IS ONE OF THE FEW POETS who has never ceased to speak to the living. Sometimes it is as the poet of a new age, at others as a poet of doom. Last century his accents were taken to be lushly romantic. Today he speaks to a generation deeply engaged upon its own 'doom-watch' and entirely sympathetic to his wit, ironies, ferocities and compassions. Perhaps for that reason we go for *Don Juan* or his inimitable letters where our predecessors swooned to the music of his love lyrics.

Adventure in fiction and fact always beckoned to him insistently; but it had to be adventure of the prescribed sort, shadowed with risk, like his long swims or his dedication to the Greek cause. Love and Byron are inseparable, especially if love is seen not as a steadfast incandescence but as a torrential experience seeping at times into the marshes of sentimentality, lust and something near to hate. The world of his imagination was doom-laden, and too often his interior sense of doom seemed to be echoed in the real world around him. When the worst happened to himself or his friends, a will o' the wisp of satisfaction gleamed over his despair. Satisfaction that life was indeed as melancholy as he had always said.

Whatever aspect of Byron may appeal to the modern reader, he or she cannot fail to be engrossed by this reappraisal of the man and his genius. Peter Brent writes with a vividness that has caught the essential flavour of his subject. By presenting his subject through a series of 'masks', he offers us, first the key to a lucid way of approaching the kaleidoscopic Byronic image – family influences, extravagances, passions, broken marriage, more sadly broken child. Second, Peter Brent uses the masks to penetrate Byron's philosophy. Put badly, this was the assertion: 'I *feel* therefore I am'. Through wearing his various masks – the young lord, the sneering public face, the sporting athlete – Byron hoped to force the world to take off its own mask, look him straight in the face and acknowledge his existence and worth. His lameness was one of the first things to drive him behind a mask. If his 'greed for women' was, as Peter Brent suggests, yet another mask through which the luminous eyes of a homosexual stared, it seems that these masks were protective as well as aggressive. And what if the homosexuality was a mask also?

When the time came for him to leave Italy for dank Missolonghi and death – a journey poignantly described by Peter Brent – we see how his last attachment (Teresa Guiccioli) painfully gave place to his last mask, that of military hero. 'But he had to go,' writes Peter Brent, – 'it was as if poetry, domesticity, sexual adventure had all ceased to stimulate. Only direct action and the chance of death remained. For if he did not feel, he did not feel he lived.'

Death finally unmasked him, showing to the perceptive world not a stage villain but a true bulwark against hypocritical tyrannies. A spirit such as Byron's must have stirred the world in whatever part of it he moved. But moving in the path of Shelley and his brilliant circle, the Melbournes including Caroline Lamb, his beloved half-sister and unloved wife, he has never ceased to produce a strong reaction. In Europe there has been no other poet's name quite like Byron's. His writings will always give delight. Whenever the tides flow towards romance and rebelliousness, he, the supreme romantic rebel, will give a voice to defiant humanity.

Elizabeth Longford

1 Boyhood

Ye scenes of my childhood, whose loved recollection
Embitters the present, compared with the past;
Where science first dawn'd on the powers of reflection,
And friendships were form'd, too romantic to last . . .

THERE IS A SENSE in which Lord Byron was always a man attempting to outrun his doom – though glancing back over his shoulder with some relish. However pleased he may sometimes have been at this vision of himself, he had reasons for conjuring it up. His lameness, his childhood poverty, the erratic behaviour of his mother, the muddle of puritanism and licentiousness in his upbringing and the well-publicised eccentricities of his forebears all helped to make his beginnings almost overwhelmingly threatening. His life thereafter seems at times like the manœuverings of a surf-rider, converting into a public and bravado beauty the force which might at any moment engulf him.

If the de Burun family were, as was supposed, the Norman ancestors of the Byrons, little is known of their fortunes until Henry VIII granted Newstead Abbey, in Nottinghamshire, to Sir John Byron. His bastard son John, knighted by Queen Elizabeth and distinguished from his father by the title 'Little Sir John with the Great Beard', was well known even in those self-indulgent days for the scale of his entertaining. Go forward almost a century, and a Byron appears again : Pepys sets down for us a piece of gossip which he had from his fellow-diarist, Evelyn, who told him that 'Lady Byron, who had been, as he called it, the King's seventeenth mistress abroad, did not leave him till she had got him to give her an order for £4000 worth of plate to be made for her; but by delays, thanks be to God! she died before she had it'.

Lord Byron's more immediate ancestors continued this tradition of extravagant behaviour. It was his grand-uncle, the fifth Lord, and not the poet, who was widely known as 'the Wicked Lord Byron': he killed a neighbour, William Chaworth, in a duel over a trivial disagreement. He built on a lake at Newstead a small castle in which, it was believed, he and his cronies took part in un-speakable orgies. Other rumours about him were more specific – that he had shot his coachman, for example, thrown his body in the coach beside his wife and driven the carriage on himself. Predictably, his wife left him and his son ran off with a cousin.

His brother, who was Byron's direct grandfather, was a sailor so notorious for attracting storms that he became known as 'Foul-weather Jack'. Having married, as the Byrons tended to, a cousin, he seems to have attracted matrimonial storms with the same frequency, apparently seeing no contradiction between his vows of conjugal fidelity and his determination to maintain and even extend his reputation as a rake.

PREVIOUS PAGES Newstead Abbey, Byron's 'fast-falling, once-resplendent dome'.

12

His son, the poet's father, however, outdid him as a spend-thrift and profligate, for his efforts earning the sobriquet 'Mad Jack Byron' and being disinherited by the admiral. Commissioned in the Guards, he served in the American colonies and returned determined, one supposes, to secure his own independence. In 1778, aged twenty-two, he met Lady Carmarthen, who being both beautiful and rich promised an avenue to freedom. Lord Carmarthen simplified Mad Jack's progress by locking his doors against his wife when he learned of their affair; with apparent equanimity, she moved in with her lover and when, the following year, Lord Carmarthen divorced her, the couple married, a month before their first daughter was born. As always when Captain Byron was near it, money responded to his ardour by melting away; soon he and his small family had to move to France to escape creditors, the evasion of whom seems to have played so large a part in the activities of the eighteenth-century aristocracy.

Though prodigal with her money, Captain Jack seems to have been reasonably faithful to his wife, but in 1784 she died while giving birth to Augusta, paradoxically the only one of her children to survive. So the next spring, Mad Jack, still the right side of thirty, appeared among the clustering heiress-hunters of Bath, a character who appears to us more out of Georgette Heyer than Jane Austen. In a very short time, practised as he was, he had

Bath, where Byron's parents met, was one of England's richest hunting-grounds for fortunes in the marriage market.

13

ABOVE Newstead Abbey,
by Pieter Tillemans.

OPPOSITE Byron and his
'protégé', Robert Rushton,
landing from a boat, by
George Sanders.

14

come across and run down his quarry: a rather plain but very rich young lady named Catherine Gordon. In May of that year, 1785, she married Jack Byron.

OPPOSITE Mrs Byron. Her husband wrote of her, 'She is very amiable at a distance; but I defy you and all the Apostles to live with her two months. . . .'

Her ancestors, too, seem to have been rather a robust collection, their eccentricities at least as great as those of the Byrons, though displayed in the more open-handed manner common among the reivers and robber-barons who thieved, rustled and raped along the Scottish border. Herself an orphan, Catherine had been brought up in strict Calvinist gloom by her grandmother, a woman who mitigated the darkness of ignorance by the spurious glitter of superstition. Catherine seems to have had a strong tendency towards manic depression, her periods of hysteria and fury being divided by bouts of introspective melancholy. Although she was shrewd in some ways and by no means stupid, she had little education and so none of the stability that a genuine depth of cultivation might have given her.

Captain Jack fell upon her fortune as he had fallen upon that of his first wife; by the end of 1786, her home in Scotland, Gight Castle, had been lived in, mortgaged, fled from and put on the market. She asked a kinswoman to intercede with the commissioners selling it; she wanted £10,000 of the money it made settled on her 'in such a manner that it would be out of Mr Byron's power to spend, and out of my own power to give up to him'. But half the sum Gight fetched ended up in the pockets of the Captain's creditors; a year later he himself had scrambled to the safety of Paris. Pregnant now, Mrs Byron followed, to discover Augusta ill, her husband once more scratching for *sous* and herself isolated by her ignorance of French. As soon as she had nursed Augusta back to health, therefore, she returned with her to England, saw her safely into the care of Lady Holderness, her grandmother, and found herself lodgings in London – a back room, furnished, respectable and cheap but tiny, in Holles Street, just off Oxford Street.

Drawn by the small allowance doled out to her from Scotland, Jack Byron followed her early in 1788. Since debtors were allowed immunity on Sundays, he became a one-day-a-week husband, arriving each week-end to squeeze or charm what money he could from Catherine, then spending the other six days in side-stepping his creditors and their agents. He is therefore unlikely to have been present – and even less likely to have regretted it – when the future Lord Byron was born, on Tuesday, 22 January 1788.

The boy was born lame. His own later secretiveness gave some

17

zest to the controversy which followed his fame wherever it was discussed, both during his lifetime and for a century after it: had he truly a club foot? The answer seems to be that he truly had. A special shoe was designed for him by John Hunter, a famous surgeon of the day, but the doctor was firm in his opinion that the condition could not be cured. And the deformity in Byron's right foot, which almost certainly determined so many of his later attitudes and actions, never was cured, though attempts were made to do so, some very painful. Nevertheless, the boy learned to accommodate himself to his condition, at least superficially, so that in the end only those pastimes which involved an extreme lightness of foot proved beyond him.

Christened George Gordon after Catherine's father, at a ceremony in February which his own father found it impossible, or not sufficiently appealing, to attend, the boy was to remain in London for only just over a year. His mother had managed to arrange that the shifting sands of her finances should be fixed once and for all, the procedure leaving her with £150 a year out of a capital, barred to Captain Jack, of £3000. With this sum now as the basis of her budgeting, Catherine took her baby back to Scotland, where the money would go further than in London. She settled in lodgings in Aberdeen; her husband, once more attracted by the scent of money in regular, if tiny, doses, joined her there. Unable to bear the restraints imposed by a poverty-stricken marriage, however, he soon moved – to the other end of the street, far enough to be free, near enough to remind Catherine of her duty to support her husband.

In the autumn of 1790, Mad Jack travelled for the last time to France. His sister owned a house in Valenciennes and he moved into it, delighting for a while the women of that place – 'As for me, here I am, and in love with whom? A new actress who is come from Paris . . .' he wrote, in phrases almost uncomfortably like those his son would use some thirty years later – only to sink for the last time under all that weight of debt, his charm in the end not sufficient to keep him afloat nor the women loving enough to warm him; in August 1792 he died. Catherine's yells of grief carried to the sober Aberdeen street beneath her windows; 'I do not think I shall ever recover the severe shock I have received,' she wrote to Mrs Leigh, her sister-in-law, and probably she never did.

Widowed mother, fatherless son and Agnes Gray, the boy's nurse, moved into a flat in Broad Street; they had a life to make,

No. 16 Holles Street, London,
where Byron was born on
22 January 1788.

now that the periodic raids of Jack Byron on the family purse had
come to an end. Mrs Byron furnished the place herself; it was large
enough for young George Gordon to have his own room and
perhaps he was glad to have some respite from the Calvinistic,
Bible-dominated Nurse Gray. There is a sort of wildness that one
senses in this household, the special madness which perhaps every
family generates in its own way. Mrs Byron veered in her relations
with her son from vituperation to kisses, swooping from one
emotion to the other with almost Slavonic abandon. In her loving
moods, she would smother him with endearments and caresses, in
her furies attack him with insults about his lameness and his
supposed similarity to his dissolute father. In the background
lurked Agnes Gray, eternal damnation at her beck and call, while
at the centre the young Byron stalked, already proud, demanding,
self-absorbed and over-sensitive, conscious of the barrier his
lameness could make between himself and the world. Agnes Gray
and he, out walking one day, were greeted by a passing nurse-

19

Aberdeen. Byron and his
mother lived there from the
summer of 1789 until 1798,
when he succeeded to the
title Baron Byron of
Rochdale.

Byron at the age of seven.

maid with the remark, 'What a pretty boy Byron is. What a pity he has such a leg!' Outraged, the child struck at her with his toy whip, ordering her not to speak of it.

When he was five, the boy was sent to his first school, a poverty-stricken establishment not far from where he lived. The contrast between the aristocracy of his origins and the plebeian nature of his surroundings became starker the following year, for in Corsica a cannonball ended the life of William Byron, grandson of the 'Wicked Lord', and made George Gordon heir presumptive to the barony and its estate of Newstead Abbey. By then, however, he had also moved up the educational ladder, becoming a pupil at Aberdeen Grammar School.

More importantly, he had discovered books. From now on, certainly throughout his youth, he was to read with an omnivorous, insatiable delight, ingesting history, tales of travel, classics, translations, novels and accounts of great deeds and battles, all at enormous speed and with a precocious intensity. Knolles's *Turkish History* was perhaps especially important, for as he said, 'I believe it had much influence on my subsequent wish to visit the Levant, and gave, perhaps, the oriental colouring which is to be observed in my poetry.' Yet poetry itself did not attract him; on the contrary, he 'could never bear to read any Poetry whatever without disgust and reluctance'.

What drew him more, as was not surprising, given the influence of both mother and nurse, was the Bible. Even the Psalms, acknowledged poems though they were, did not deter him. The story of Cain and Abel already fascinated him; the idea of evil done under compulsion, of the man cursed – 'a fugitive and a vagabond shalt thou be in the earth' – seemed even at that age to awake a strange resonance within him. Perhaps he felt already the beginnings of that certainty of doom which dominated him, to his horror and delight, throughout most of his life.

Another strand in that dark tapestry was woven in when he was around nine years old. Agnes Gray left the Byrons; in her stead, her younger sister May entered the household. May, who remained in the household until Byron was twelve, was as devout and Bible-quoting as her sister. Not only that, she ordered the boy's life by beatings so violent that in the later words of Hanson, the Byrons' London agent, 'his bones sometimes ached from it'. But there was another element in May's character. Much later, in his 'Detached Thoughts', Byron wrote, 'My passions were developed early – so early, that few would believe me, if I were to state the period, and the facts which accompanied it.' For, in Hanson's words, when Byron was nine, 'a free Scotch girl used to come to bed to him and play tricks with his person'. Thus aroused, however, Byron discovered that he was only on the periphery of her sensual world (she having, in those circumstances, to stand at the centre of his), for Hanson reported that 'she brought all sorts of Company of the very lowest Description into his apartments'. Thus he had not only to learn feeling and response, to cope with the frightening excitement of an adult and to match it as best he could with his own, he had also to watch that effort spurned, that gift nullified, as in his presence May entertained her uninhibited friends.

It was not uncommon, until well into this century, for the youths of the middle and upper classes to be sexually initiated by

A fountain in the Cloister Garth, at Newstead Abbey.

older servants; one only has to read the 'Histories of Sexual Development' in Havelock Ellis's *Psychology of Sex* to realise that this was the case. What harm this did, and whether it outweighed the benefits, it is hard to say. What is certain is that, coupled as it was with both Calvinistic prohibitions of carnality and a repeated violence to enforce them, Byron's initiation does much to explain his subsequent sexual confusion. That beyond all this stood only his irascible, unstable mother meant that he had nowhere to turn for reassurance; the damage done to his emotions had no one to repair it. And it never was repaired.

Perhaps equally significant in determining the shape of his life was that, when he was ten, his grandfather died and he became Lord Byron. Mrs Byron at once brought her son back to England,

24

arriving at Newstead Abbey, the family seat near Nottingham, with a capital of some £75, realised on the sale of her Broad Street furniture. She had hoped for an income of £2000 a year, but instead learned from Hanson that the estate was chained by the old lord's debts; most of the furniture had been taken by creditors, cattle had been given the entrance hall as a byre, the farm buildings were tumbling into ruin, the forests had been decimated. If she had expected a life of ease and fortune, she was quickly disillusioned.

Yet she, and especially her son, fell in love with Newstead. It stood, romantic Gothic and sturdy Tudor, beside its lakes, within its wide parkland, framed by the dark green of the late-summer trees. For a boy whose imagination had already been quickened by a thousand tales of ancient battles, it must have seemed a paradise, especially after the constraints of Aberdeen. It was decided, despite Hanson's doubts, that the family could live at Newstead, at least until someone could be found to rent it.

Hanson, a shrewd man much concerned for the young Byron, saw quite quickly that the boy, disturbed by the unpredictable tantrums and kisses of his mother, was in danger of wasting an obvious potential. In July 1799 he brought the boy back to his house in London. He worked hard on Byron's behalf, taking him to eminent surgeons and seeing to it that, when hope of cure failed, a special boot was designed to lessen his lameness as far as possible. At the same time he organised a petition to the King which resulted in Mrs Byron's receiving a Civil List pension of £300 a year. With this income to call on, Hanson put the boy in a school in Dulwich run by a Dr Glennie, familiarly Scottish. But soon Mrs Byron was in London, lodging in Sloane Terrace; only a little later, Byron himself was back at Newstead with her. It was as though they needed this proximity, however violent the emotions it provoked. Once, when Dr Glennie remonstrated with her for allowing Byron to stay away from school for such long stretches, she became furious in a manner audible all over the building. 'Byron, your mother is a fool,' said one of his classmates. One can hear the resigned sigh in his words as he answered, 'I know it.'

A boarding school seemed to Hanson the only remedy for the damage this relationship was doing Byron. Using the good offices of Byron's kinsman, Lord Carlisle, who had been helpful both in the efforts to find a cure for Byron's lameness and in the petition to the King, Hanson managed to get the boy interviewed and then

Byron in Harrow churchyard.
*Again I behold where for
   hours I have ponder'd,
As reclining, at eve, on
   yon tombstone I lay . . .*

26

accepted by Dr Drury, the Headmaster of Harrow. 'There is another boy, Ld. Byram, a lame fellow just come, he seems a good sort of fellow,' wrote a schoolboy appraisingly of the new arrival. And by and large, once the early battles for acceptance were over – true battles, some of them: Byron claimed he won six of his first seven fights – Byron became popular at Harrow. After the first term, when he found it difficult to settle, he discovered much that was congenial to him there; boredom with the education offered was its main drawback. He refused to accept any

but the most insistent of the limitations his lameness imposed on him; thus he fought and he played a fair game of cricket – he was one of the Harrow eleven in their first match against Eton in 1805, though according to another member of the team he had a runner, 'his lameness impeding him so much'; above all, he swam, having taken several years before with a pleasure one can imagine to an element in which he could start level with the rest of the world.

He began to write verses, began to spend long day-dreaming hours, withdrawn from his friends, shadowed by the elms of Harrow churchyard. While the dreary business of poring over the texts of long-dead Greeks palled, and he was often bored with the school, he yet began there a number of relationships which, if they did not all last very long after his schooldays were over, yet taught him in some sense the habit of friendship (and possibly more). Tutored by Dr Drury's son Henry, his formal studies improved. 'I have been placed in a higher form in this School to day,' he wrote to his mother on 23 June 1803. Dr Drury realised early that in Byron he had a pupil with abilities which, though ill-defined, were clear. 'He has talents, my lord, which will add lustre to his rank,' he enthused to Lord Carlisle. 'Indeed!', grunted his lordship, noncommitally.

Newstead was let to Lord Grey de Ruthyn and Mrs Byron moved to Southwell, also near Nottingham, where, in a house called Burbage Manor, Byron joined her for the summer. Quickly bored, however, he moved back to Newstead, established himself in the caretaker's lodge – and fell in love. He had been in love before, the first time before he was ten, with a girl named Mary Duff. In 1813 he was to write in his diary, 'How very odd that I should have been so utterly, devotedly fond of that girl, at an age when I could neither feel passion, nor know the meaning of the word. . . . I recollect all we said to each other, all our caresses, her features, my restlessness. . . .' A little later, he had fallen in love again with his cousin Margaret Parker, who, as he was to write in his 'Detached Thoughts', inspired his 'first dash into poetry'; she had been, he added, 'one of the most beautiful of evanescent beings. . . . Her dark eyes! Her long eye-lashes! her completely Greek cast of face and figure! . . . I do not recollect scarcely any thing equal to the *transparent* beauty of my cousin. . . . I could not sleep, could not eat; I could not rest . . . it was the torture of my life to think of the time which must elapse before we could meet again – being usually about *twelve hours* of separation! But I was a

OPPOSITE Byron as a boy. He wrote to his mother upon leaving for Harrow, 'the way *to riches, to greatness* lies before me. I can, I will cut myself a path through the world, or perish in the attempt.'

Mary Chaworth.
'She was the *beau idéal* of all
that my youthful fancy
could paint of beautiful; and
I have taken all my fables
about the celestial nature of
women from the perfection
my imagination created in
her – I say created, for I
found her, like the rest of
the sex, anything but
angelic.'

fool then, and am not much wiser now.' He had been twelve
then; a year or so later, Margaret was dead, a blow the boy felt,
pondered on, then drew into himself as though to nourish his
more melancholy moods.

This time, the girl he fell in love with was the daughter of a
neighbour and the descendant of his grand-uncle's victim: Mary
Chaworth. So profound was the fall that nothing would induce
him to go back to Harrow when the summer was over. 'I cannot
get him to return to school,' wailed Mrs Byron in a letter to
Hanson. 'He has no indisposition that I know of, but love,
desperate love. . . .' Miss Chaworth, for her part, already engaged
to a neighbour, seems for a while to have been flattered by the
distracted state of this good-looking if slightly corpulent fifteen-
year-old schoolboy; if nothing else, at least her vanity was
excited. But one night she apparently said to her maid, 'What!
Me care for that lame boy!' Byron overhead her or was told of it
and, wounded to fury, rushed out of the house.

The unattainable, utterly beautiful, totally romantic – dead
Margaret and scornful Mary; one pattern for love had been
established. Perfection involved distance and those with whom he
was never able to close that distance rode on in Byron's mind,
ghosts given perhaps his truest, because his most unfleshly,
devotion. At Harrow, the same pattern had been established, in a
way, for while his emotions were deeply involved in his friendships there – 'My School friendships were with me *passions* (for I
was always violent)' he wrote years later – it is quite probable
that they were given no physical expression, although usually
with younger boys of noticeable beauty. Not that this can be
absolutely certain if one remembers the turbulence of schoolboy
sexuality, especially when it is locked up within the walls and
rules of a boarding school; any number of confessional novels
and autobiographies have since testified to the widely accepted
homosexuality in many public schools. Yet there is a feeling of a
remembered purity (however wrapped in deep emotions and
whether a cover for an unacknowledged sexuality or not) about
the words in which Byron, not a reticent or an untruthful man,
described the relationships which brightened his schooldays.

That he was not over-familiar with homosexuality, or that its
clearer manifestations frightened and disgusted him at this stage
in his life, seems to be shown in his precipitate flight from his
beloved Newstead, where he had remained as a companion to
Lord Grey, the young tenant there. For it seems more than likely

that Lord Grey, himself only twenty-three, made physical advances to his good-looking young companion, in a manner sufficiently gross to bewilder and alarm him. He left there, telling no one why, but repeating his determination never to have anything to do with Lord Grey again. 'I am not reconciled to Lord Grey, *and I never will be*,' he wrote to his sister Augusta; but he added that 'my reasons for ceasing that Friendship are such as I cannot explain, not even to you. . . .'

Thus struggling in the emotional thickets of adolescence he found little support in his mother. As he wrote to Augusta, after having provoked her wrath by criticising Southwell, 'I assure you upon my *honour*, jesting apart, I have never been so *scurrilously*, and *violently* abused by any person, as by that person, whom I think I am to call mother. . . . I disclaim her from this time, and although I cannot help treating her with respect, I cannot reverence, as I ought to, that parent who by her outrageous conduct forfeits all title to filial affection.'

It was in this final year to Harrow that he turned, not to its formal institutionalised side, but to the comradeship and admiration it now afforded him. At seventeen years of age, he was one of its leading lights, a young man in a world of boys, looked up to and respected for his disdain of its authority. He led a small rebellion against the new headmaster appointed to succeed the retiring Dr Drury. He played cricket (it was the year he was picked against

Byron's dog Boatswain. When Boatswain died, Byron had him buried in the grounds at Newstead.
To mark a friend's remains
*   these stones arise;*
I never knew but one, – and
*   here he lies.*

Eton), he sang at the nearby tavern, he dazzled at the end-of-term Speech Day. Having found a place, having wrested respect from those about him, perhaps like many school heroes he was afraid of the colder world outside. So wrought up was he about leaving, that, as he wrote later, 'it broke my rest for the last quarter with counting the days that remained'.

Yet those days dribbled away, as they had to; at the beginning of July 1805, he had written to Augusta, 'I am just returned from Cambridge, where I have been to enter myself at Trinity College.' By the autumn, he had made the transition from school to university and was installed in rooms on Trinity's Great Court. He was to be happy at Cambridge, yet as he grew older he was to realise that his attachment to Harrow had been in some ways the most important of his early youth. As he wrote some fifteen years later in 'Detached Thoughts', 'When I first went up to College, it was a new and a heavy hearted scene for me . . . it was one of the deadliest and heaviest feelings of my life to feel that I was no longer a boy. From that moment I began to grow old in my own esteem: and in my esteem age is not estimable.'

2 Discovery

Now at last we're off for Turkey,
    Lord knows when we shall come back!
Breezes foul and tempests murky
    May unship us in a crack.

FOR BYRON, AS FOR SO MANY OTHERS, university meant not education so much as self-discovery. What he discovered, of course, was not always to his liking. Yet he was happy with his new liberty – 'I am allowed 500 a year, a Servant and Horse, so Feel as independent as a German Prince who coins his own cash,' he wrote to Augusta late in 1805. However, as he was to write later in 'Detached Thoughts', 'I took my gradations in the vices with great promptitude, but they were not to my taste . . . though my temperament was naturally burning, I could not share in the common place libertinism of the place and time without disgust.' Nevertheless libertinism, however it may have disgusted him, proved expensive and he was soon in money trouble, writing high-handed letters to Hanson, trying to induce his sister to stand security with him 'for a few Hundreds a person (one of the money lending tribe) has offered to advance' and contracting debts and collecting unpayable bills in the manner of any grandee.

One has the feeling that, quite apart from his personal inclinations, he also felt that such behaviour was correct for the role he had been called on to play, that of 'the young lord'. Coming to the part a little late and somewhat unexpectedly, there is a sense throughout his life of its mannerisms, gestures and demands being almost consciously produced. He had, perhaps, found the first of the masks he was to wear, those intricate façades, their grimaces formidable and exaggerated, which he was to flaunt throughout his life to the astonishment, censure or admiration of the bystanders.

Cambridge palled; London beckoned. He ran through more money, raised a new sum. He returned to Cambridge. In 1806 he came home to Southwell, but found no way – there is little indication that he tried hard – of placating his mother. He was in London again, then in Brighton, staying with his Harrow friend, Edward Noel Long (it was he who had written at his Harrow arrival that 'he seems a good sort of fellow'). In September he was back in Southwell, doubtless quarrelling with his mother, yet managing to bear her, and acting in the private theatricals which were the delight of his friends there, the Pigots. (Elizabeth Pigot, some years older than he, was for a long time one of that group of confidantes – Augusta, Hobhouse, Lady Melbourne, Thomas Moore – without whom as audience Byron seemed to value neither sentiment nor action.) Yet for all his travelling to and fro, for all his dissipation, his light-hearted and even cynical *amours*, his spendthrift and easy generosity, Byron cannot have been entirely idle, for in November, under the title *Fugitive Pieces*, his first volume of poetry appeared, privately printed and handed as gifts to his friends.

The poems caused a certain Puritan consternation, although most of them were innocuous, academic, bland and rather bad. However, such lines as

> Now, by my soul, 'tis most delight
> To view each other panting, dying,
> In love's *exstatic* posture lying. . .

were not calculated to win clerical approval. Byron, astonished at the outcry, and always sensitive to any adverse opinion he had not deliberately provoked, called in most of the copies he had presented to his friends and burned them. To John Pigot he wrote that he was preparing a new volume, 'vastly correct and miraculously chaste'. *Poems on Various Occasions* appeared in 1807, like the previous collection privately printed in a limited edition, no more than a rich man's whim.

That he was not a rich man, of course, he knew very well; his affairs became more and more complicated, with borrowed money going to pay older debts, and promises to pay when he came of age writing off prodigious future sums in interest. Nor were these his only problems, for he had also decided to slim. He had for most of his life so far been a rather portly youth; when he was eighteen he weighed over 200 lbs, almost dangerously heavy for someone not five feet nine inches tall. 'I wear *seven* Waistcoats and a great Coat, run, and play at cricket in this Dress, till quite exhausted by excessive perspiration . . . no Suppers or Breakfast, only one Meal a Day. . . .' This regime produced results, however, for he added that 'my Clothes have been taken in nearly *half a yard*'.

He saw his future at this time as in politics and thought of himself as an orator. His title would give him automatic entry to the legislature when he came of age and he intended, once in the House of Lords, to speak for the more liberal factions of the Whig Party; later in 1807, he became a member of the Whig Club at Cambridge. In these oratorical ambitions, Hanson enthusiastically encouraged him.

What Cambridge meant for Byron, in the meantime, was more than anything else the companionship he found there. Like so many others, he forged friendships while a student which, although usually less passionate than those he had formed at Harrow, lasted the whole of his life. The most important of these was with the son of a Bristol MP, John Cam Hobhouse (later Lord Broughton) who, like Byron, saw politics from a liberal standpoint; he held the ambition to enter the House of Commons as his father had done. Hobhouse, however, though loyal, intelligent and lively, was limited by a slightly conventional narrowness in his opinions. When Byron wanted the freedom of untrammelled speculation, allowing thought and imagination to lead the conversation to whatever lengths it would, it was to a friend of Hobhouse's that he turned, Skinner Matthews. It may be that Matthews on occasion shocked even Byron, for he later described him as 'a most decided atheist, indeed noxiously so, for he proclaimed his principles in all societies'.

But an attachment very different from these was, in some ways, more significant than either. Byron met and became passionately involved with a young chorister, John Edleston, whom he heard singing in the College chapel the first autumn he was in Cambridge. It was, Byron later said, 'a violent, though *pure*, love and passion'. Yet it was certainly a love affair, the first of many such in Byron's life, not all of which were to remain in the technical sense 'pure'.

If in the unknown layers of his psyche he hated women, it would not have been surprising, and from one point of view his life can be taken as a long odyssey of revenge against them. The family configuration of demanding mother and absent father is of course the classical one for the moulding of a homosexual. Thus a part of Byron's apparent greed for women may also have been rooted in the energy of his flight from men, may at times even have been a deliberate mask to deceive the world – another moulded grimace, that of the indiscriminate but heterosexual lecher, behind which the more loving, but homosexual, aspect of the true Byron could hide.

He wrote of Edleston to Elizabeth Pigot and described him: 'He is nearly my height, very *thin*, very fair of complexion, dark eyes and light locks.' They spent many evenings together; Edleston presented Byron with a heart-shaped cornelian.

> He offer'd it with downcast look,
>   As *fearful* that I might refuse it;
> I told him, when the gift I took,
>   My *only fear* should be, to lose it. . .

Thus Byron described the giving of that present. To Elizabeth he wrote in 1807:

He has been my *almost constant* associate since October, 1805, when I

Byron at Cambridge.
'As might be supposed I like
a College Life extremely,
especially as I have escaped
the Trammels or rather
Fetters of my domestic
Tyrant Mrs Byron.'

39

entered Trinity College. His *voice* first attracted my attention, his *countenance* fixed it, and his *manners* attached me to him for ever. . . . I certainly love him more than any human being, and neither time nor distance have had the least effect on my (in general) changeable disposition. . . . During the whole of my residence at Cambridge we met every day, summer and winter. . . .

After Edleston had left Cambridge, Byron contemplated leaving himself, but changed his mind. In the summer, he was in London – 'I swam in the Thames from Lambeth through the two bridges, Westminster and Blackfriars, a distance . . . of three miles' – and

London in the early
nineteenth century. Nash's
Regent Street Quadrant.

busy with a new poem on Bosworth Field. In this he was encouraged by the early, if moderate, success of his first volume of
poems to be brought out for public distribution, *Hours of Idleness*:
'In every Bookseller's I see my *own name*, and *say nothing*, but
enjoy my *fame* in *secret*.'

In the autumn of 1807 he was writing to Miss Pigot, 'I have
written 214 pages of a novel, – one poem of 380 lines, to be
published (without my name) in a few weeks, with notes, – 560
lines of Bosworth Field, and 250 lines of another poem. . . . The
poem to be published is a Satire.' One wonders at his energy, for

41

the letter begins, 'Fatigued with sitting up till four in the morning for the last two days at hazard. . . .'

The satirical poem 'to be published in a few weeks', *English Bards, and Scotch Reviewers*, in fact came out in March 1809. By that time Byron was permanently installed in London, his Cambridge years to be perpetuated by the friendships he had formed there, rather than by the knowledge or the qualifications he had gained. The obligatory degree he went back for in the summer of 1808 meant less to him than the opinion held of him by Hobhouse, Matthews and the rest of his close associates. In his memory, Cambridge was to be notable only for their sakes – and for that of Edleston.

Very soon, although his shortage of money remained as relentless as ever, Byron was deep in the life of a rake-about-town, aided by such dissolute wits as Scrope Davies, whom he had met at Cambridge in Matthews's company. He wrote to Hobhouse, 'I am buried in an abyss of Sensuality.' He described an evening – 'we supped with seven whores, a *Bawd* and a *Ballet master*' – and, in a later note, assured him, 'I am still living with my Delilah, who has only two faults, unpardonable in a woman – she can read and write.' He became friendly with the pugilists whose ritualised bravery so fascinated the wilder fringes of the early-nineteenth-century aristocracy; but recognising with rare common sense that he had not the funds for it, he gave up gambling, though remaining friendly with gamblers (he thought them 'as happy as most people, being always *excited*').

In January 1809, Byron celebrated his twenty-first birthday; coming of age made him eligible to take his seat in the House of Lords. In March, however, his attack on the literati of the day came out:

> Prepare for rhyme – I'll publish, right or wrong:
> Fools are my theme, let Satire be my song.

English Bards, and Scotch Reviewers had come pouring out of him, a lava-like retort to some of the criticism to which *Hours of Idleness* had finally been subjected. He made Jeffrey, editor of the *Edinburgh Review*, that stern arbiter of literary acceptability, his especial butt; it was only just over a year that this journal had written of his first volume, 'So far from hearing, with any degree of surprise, that very poor verses were written by a youth from his leaving school to his leaving college, inclusive, we really believe this to be the most common of all occurrences; that it happens in the life of nine men in ten who are educated in England and that the tenth man writes better verse than Lord Byron.' But Byron also struck out at Sir Walter Scott, at Wordsworth, at Southey and Coleridge, as well as at a varied gallery of second-raters, largely forgotten now by all except the expert pedants of the thesis mills – as are, it must be admitted, most of those whom Byron picked out to praise.

Although Byron had by now taken his seat in the House of Lords, he was already planning a voyage to the East. He put Hanson under pressure to find the necessary money; then, with several of his friends, he retired to Newstead, where a series of slightly over-heated evenings – they dressed as friars and Matthews dubbed Byron 'The Abbot' – gave rise to excited rumours in the locality. Perhaps more interesting was that Byron had taken as his page the handsome young Robert Rushton, another in that series of good-looking lads upon whom Byron expended some of his most sincere affection.

By bullying Hanson and borrowing from both usurers and friends – Scrope Davies, lucky at the gaming tables, lent him nearly £5000 – Byron finally put himself into a financial posture to depart. Hobhouse was the only one of his friends who accepted his invitation to accompany him. There is a mysterious urgency in Byron's determination to leave the country. 'I will never live in England if I can avoid it,' he wrote to Hanson. '*Why* – must remain a secret. . . .' This is strange in a man little given to secrecy and may refer to some homosexual entanglement, or at least temptation. In any event, on 2 July 1809, he had his wish, as he and Hobhouse stood on the deck of the Lisbon Packet, the *Princess Elizabeth*, and watched Falmouth and the coast of England fade into hazy summer and the past.

> And then, it may be, of his wish to roam
> Repented he, but in his bosom slept
> The silent thought. . .

If these were really his feelings, as he suggests in *Childe Harold's Pilgrimage*, they were soon to change; he was not a man to remain inert under the stimulus of the new, the beautiful and the exotic.

A fortnight in Lisbon, during which he swam the River Tagus, left Byron once more restless. He, Hobhouse and Robert Rushton travelled overland to Seville – 'we rode seventy miles a day.

43

Eggs and wine, and hard beds, are all the accommodation we found' – and then to Cadiz, which he thought 'the prettiest and sweetest town in Europe'. After a brief intrigue with the daughter of an admiral, Byron and his companions moved on to Gibraltar, where he awaited his luggage and Fletcher, his servant. Before journeying on, he sent Rushton home, insisting that Turkey was 'in too dangerous a state for boys to enter'; one assumes he had the country's internal stability in mind.

Malta, then – and Mrs Constance Spencer Smith. She was, possibly, the first woman not servant, actress or *demi-mondaine* to respond to him. Although they seem never to have become lovers, he later wrote to Lady Melbourne that he had been 'seized with an *everlasting* passion' which he thought much more violent than that which he was to feel for Lady Caroline Lamb. He made an arrangement to elope with this strange, soulful-looking lady to Friuli, but was thwarted by Napoleon's armies, which had taken the town. Promising to return after a year, Byron left and travelled on to Prevesa; then later loves and hundreds of fascinating miles pressed his feeling for her into a dry image of itself, as a flower is pressed in a great book. Their passion was to remain for ever unconsummated.

The absolute ruler of Albania was a white-bearded tyrant

Ali Pasha and his retinue
on a lake.
Ali reclined, a man of war
and woes:
Yet in his lineaments ye
cannot trace,
While Gentleness her
milder radiance throws
Along that aged venerable
face,
The deeds that lurk beneath,
and stain him with disgrace.

named Ali Pasha, whose domains extended over Macedonia and western Greece. His capital was at Jannina, and there Byron and Hobhouse arrived on 5 October, to find that quarters had already been prepared for them (in what is now 'Byron Street'). Ali Pasha, who had gone to Tepelene to confound his refractory enemies, had left word asking Byron to follow him there. So, having bought himself some gold-embroidered Albanian costumes for fifty guineas each, and been presented to Ali Pasha's grandsons, Byron, with Hobhouse, set off for Tepelene. The seventy-five miles took them a week, for heavy rains had destroyed the roads; unlike Hobhouse, Byron found the journey exhilarating, his delight brought to a new pitch by the descent from the barbaric wilderness of the mountains to the barbaric splendour of the minareted town and its crowded court. 'Amidst no common pomp the Despot sate,' he was to write in *Childe Harold's Pilgrimage*, and to match such high and bedizened state he appeared himself in a splendid staff-officer's uniform, complete with sabre. He must, one assumes, have

Byron and his party arrived at Jannina on 5 October 1809. The town, with its domes and minarets rising out of cypress groves and gardens of orange and lemon trees, was picturesquely set on a lake, with the mountains of Pindus rising abruptly from its shores.

seemed almost as exotic to the men of that mountain-protected court as they did to him and, while Ali Pasha's welcome for him was partly based on politics and an awareness that the English were becoming more and more powerful in the Eastern Mediterranean, there is no doubt that the self-indulgent ruler took a great fancy to him. To his mother, Byron wrote, 'The vizier received me in a large room, paved with marble; a fountain was playing in the centre. . . . He received me standing . . . and made me sit down on his right hand. . . . He said he was certain I was a man of birth, because I had small ears, curling hair, and little white hands. . . . He begged me to visit him often, and at night, when he was at leisure.' Whatever his mother thought of it, it is unlikely that Byron was really unaware of the slightly ambiguous overtones in the Pasha's praise of him. He could see the old ruler quite objectively, however, and called him 'as barbarous as he is successful'.

After two further visits to Ali Pasha, Byron returned to Jannina and there, on the last day of October, sat down to write the opening lines of his long poem, *Childe Harold's Pilgrimage*. An extended effort at transmuting experience almost immediately into art, this work marked the first appearance of the true 'Byronic' hero in Byron's writings (though he had already appeared in the writings of others, most notably Schiller's).

Three days later, Byron was on the move again, travelling in one of Ali's ships. This soon found itself gripped helplessly in one of the squalls which blow up so abruptly in those seas: 'Fletcher yelled after his wife, the Greeks called on all the saints, the Mussulmans on Alla; the captain burst into tears,' he wrote to his mother, and added that he himself, wrapped in his Albanian cloak, 'lay down on deck to await the worst'. This not occurring, Byron and his companions changed ships and by 20 November had reached Missolonghi. A dull town on a marshy lagoon, it made no discernible impression on the poet; if for a moment premonition stirred his skin or caused a hesitation in his blood, he did not record it.

On the way to Athens, Byron and his party stayed at Vostitza, with the Governor of the district, a wealthy Greek named Andreas Londos who, although a servant of the Turks, jumped up with tears in his eyes at the mention of a Greek nationalist who some two decades earlier had led a revolt against Turkish rule. Was this the first time that Byron understood the depth of hatred in which the Greeks held their Turkish overlords, the desperation with which they longed to be free of the bonds of the decaying, yet still

A group of Turkish soldiers near the Acropolis, Athens. *Where'er we tread, 'tis haunted, holy ground . . .*

strong, Ottoman Empire? Somehow, in retrospect, the moment seems significant, this wealthy young man, correct, charged by the Turks with responsibility, an example of co-operation between master and mastered, suddenly upright, his eyes bright with tears, his hands clasped in passionate greeting for no more than the name of a dead patriot and, watching him, the English traveller, ready to be moved by a cause rooted in liberty – and in a culture not his own. 'Rise Up, O Greeks!' Londos sang, words which were to work as fatally on Byron's heart as any arrow of Cupid's.

Delphi, Parnassus, finally Athens; Byron delighted in the relic-ridden landscape, 'Land of lost Gods and godlike men'. He and Hobhouse rode into Athens at Christmas 1809, and found

lodgings in the house of a widow, Mrs Macri, whose husband had been the British Vice-Consul. Soon it became clear that the three young daughters of the household, and especially the youngest, Theresa, had begun to divert his attention from the patiently waiting Mrs Spencer Smith. Theresa was at that time only twelve, and for this as well as other reasons out of Byron's immediate reach, but he felt for her some of the same idealised passion which was sometimes kindled in him by boys. That side of his nature, however, was also soon to be active, for when Hobhouse returned to Athens in February, after some three weeks' excursion on his own, he found Byron had installed as protégé a fifteen-year-old boy, Nicolo Giraud.

Yet the most demanding passion of this period and perhaps of his whole life was his burgeoning and developing love for Greece. He had a hatred of coercion, and for the first time in his life was witnessing the harshness of a long-established imperialism. Distanced from his fellow-countrymen by so much – his title, his lameness, his erstwhile poverty, his sexual precocity and homosexual proclivities, perhaps above all by his intelligence, cool, detached and tilted towards scepticism – he might well have

LEFT Theresa Macri, the 'Maid of Athens'. Though he immortalised her in his poem, Byron later wrote to Hobhouse, 'The old woman, Theresa's mother, was mad enough to imagine I was going to marry the girl; but I have better amusement.'

ABOVE Smyrna. 'I smoke, and stare at mountains, and twirl my mustachios very independently. I miss no comforts, and the mosquitoes that rack the morbid frame of H. [Hobhouse] have, luckily for me, little effect on mine . . .'

needed another, nobler sort of patriotism. Greece provided it, or seemed to, and her cause more and more possessed him.

Nevertheless, he did not allow this to interfere too much with either his sight-seeing or his other, pleasanter activities. He would ride every day with Hobhouse; in the evenings, there was dancing and horseplay at the house of Mrs Macri, with her three daughters in ebullient evidence. There were visitors from the more familiar parts of Europe to speak to, or to meet; there was a number of 'Frankish' families who lived in Athens and could be visited; there was, finally, the endless strangeness of this ancient, formidably foreign city, with its thousands of Turks and its continuous, almost Asiatic, hubbub. When the opportunity came, however, to move on, he remembered his determination to journey to Constantinople; offered passage on the British frigate *Pylades*, he took it at a day's notice; by the first week in March, he and Hobhouse were in Smyrna, on the mainland of Asia Minor. Here, waiting to continue his journey, he finished the Second Canto of *Childe Harold's Pilgrimage*.

By 14 April, on board the frigate *Salsette*, Byron was in sight of the Hellespont, but held there by contrary winds. He explored the

49

A view of Constantinople;
from a nineteenth-century
engraving.

plain on which Troy had stood, insisting like an early Schliemann on the authenticity of Homer. With Lieutenant Ekenhead, he swam Leander's classical route across the Hellespont: 'the current renders it hazardous,' he wrote to a friend, '– so much so that I doubt whether Leander's conjugal affection must not have been a little chilled in his passage to Paradise.' Despite the banter, this was a feat in which Byron was to take a lifelong pride. At this time, too, perhaps having been given time for reflection by the long wait in the Dardanelles, he wrote to his Cambridge friend, Hodgson, 'I begin to find out that nothing but virtue will do in this damned world. I am tolerably sick of vice. . . .' On his return, he added, he would 'leave off wine and carnal company, and betake myself to politics and decorum'.

By mid-May, Byron had arrived in Constantinople; not much given to painting word-pictures of his surroundings, he referred Hodgson to Gibbon's description of the city, 'very correct as far as I have seen'. What he himself looked like at the time was set down by an unknown author and published more than a dozen years later in *The New Monthly Magazine*: 'He wore a scarlet coat, richly embroidered with gold. . . . His features were remarkably delicate, and would have given him a feminine appearance, but for the manly expression of his fine blue eyes.' Taking off his feathered, cocked hat, he revealed 'curly auburn hair, which improved in no small degree the uncommon beauty of his face'. Dazzling, then, vain, perhaps over-aware of himself, yet well armed to command attention, it was this Byron who presented himself to Robert Adair, the British Ambassador, and who wandered, gaudy and self-possessed, through the mosques and brash bazaars of this ancient megapolis. He called the Turkish burial grounds 'the loveliest spots on earth' and added, to his mother, 'I never beheld a work of nature or art which yielded an impression like the prospect on each side from the Seven Towers to the end of the Golden Horn'. Yet Constantinople bored him; Turks he found less appealing than Greeks, perhaps because he spoke no Turkish. He quarrelled with Adair over a matter of his placing in a procession – Byron was always very conscious of what he felt was due to his rank – then was mollified by a dinner. He rode out into the country. He went with Adair to an audience with the Sultan – and unaccountably says nothing of the splendour of that court, perhaps because, as Leslie A. Marchand suggests in his biography, he could not in such a throng make any individual mark. When Adair left for England, Byron was on the frigate – not

PREVIOUS PAGES The mosque
of Sultan Ahmet, the
so-called Blue Mosque, in
Constantinople.

ABOVE Sultan Mahmut II
gave the British Ambassador,
in whose retinue Byron was,
an audience which, for all
its splendour and pageantry,
failed to impress Byron as
Ali Pasha's simpler
audiences had.

yet on his way home himself, but returning to the Greece to which
he had lost his heart, the Near East now apparently forgotten. It
was Hobhouse who had come to the end of his wanderings and was
going back to England.

Perhaps because of their imminent parting, Byron seemed very
depressed during this voyage. It may be, however, that he was
brooding over news he had had from England, where there were
not only continuing problems with creditors, but where his
erstwhile 'Cornelian', Edleston, had been accused of indecency.
This black ending to a 'pure', if passionate, attachment might well
have raised strange guilts and spectres in his mind. On 17 July,

Byron was once more on the soil of Greece, his farewells to Hobhouse said, a small bunch of flowers sentimentally divided between them, the parting suffered and over, the world now open to his solitary attack. For there seems little question that the more conservative, shockable Hobhouse had to some extent forced Byron to limit his social and sexual experimentation. It is likely that, alone, he now felt able to behave with a new and total freedom. As he later wrote in his journal, Hobhouse 'don't know what I was about the year after he left the Levant; nor does anyone'. But wily friends know more about one than one supposes, and Hobhouse's note in the margins of Moore's later biography of Byron – 'He has not the remotest grasp of the real reason which induced Lord Byron to prefer having no Englishman immediately and constantly near him' – suggests that he had a clear idea of the areas of darkness, inner and outer, which Byron preferred to explore alone.

What were they? It is hard not to conclude that it was the homosexual elements in his complex nature to which he at least half-wanted to give rein. Hobhouse, who had been with him, joyful in friar's robes, during the mildly orgiastic nights at Newstead, did not have to be turned away from the sight of Byron in the arms of maids or actresses or whores. Certainly, in Athens Byron found that the charms of Mrs Macri's daughters had waned; there was some pressure, a suggestion even of marriage, 'but I have better amusement,' he wrote to Hobhouse. He travelled to Vostitza again and once more stayed with the Governor, Andreas Londos. And there he took under his protection a youth he had come across before, Eustathios Georgiu – 'my dearly-beloved Eustathios, ready to follow me not only to England, but to Terra Incognita. . . . The next morning I found the dear soul upon horseback clothed very sprucely in Greek Garments, with those ambrosial curls hanging down his amiable back, and . . . a *parasol* in his hand to save his complexion from the heat. However, in spite of the *Parasol* on we travelled very much enamoured. . . .' Thus Byron to Hobhouse, laughing at his own obsession, yet by the laughter with its implied embarrassment and its touch of defiance confirming that the obsession was real.

The place they travelled on to was Tripolitza, where Veli Pasha, Ali Pasha's son, held court. Son proved to have the same taste as father, and Byron was rather embarrassed, though flattered too, as the long-bearded Veli held his hand, put his arm round his waist or offered him a variety of gifts. 'He . . . hoped that we should

be on good terms, not for a few days but for life,' Byron wrote to Hobhouse. Soon came a multiple parting of the ways, however; Eustathios, too demanding and apparently subject to epileptic fits, was returned to his father, while Byron himself made his way back to Athens. He left the Macri household for good, somewhat disenchanted with Theresa (who, like others to come, nevertheless enjoyed for life the fame of one who had elicited Lord Byron's passion) and settled, perhaps oddly, in a Capuchin monastery at the foot of the Acropolis.

The probable reason for this choice was his old favourite, Nicolo Giraud, who was one of six pupils living in the monastery, in the care of the Abbot. All six of the boys seem to have romped in a distinctly flirtatious manner with Byron; he called them his

Byron's Capuchin monastery in Athens. 'I am most auspiciously settled in the Convent,' he wrote to Hobhouse on 23 August 1810. 'We have nothing but riot from noon to night.'

'sylphs'. But it was Nicolo to whom he was especially drawn, needing to involve himself, perhaps, happy to feel love in an un-complicated way; as Byron told Hobhouse, Nicolo had said that he would follow him across the world and that they should not only live but die together: 'The latter I hope to avoid – as much of the former as he pleases.' He was, he added, 'vastly happy and childish'. Confirmed by another's affection, his existence and lovability thus certified, Byron was always happy – especially perhaps when the circumstances reproduced the easy, unre-peatable 'passions' of his Harrow days. The monastery must, for a while, have seemed like his old school, with Nicolo to play the part of a Clare or a Long.

He swam daily at Piraeus; returning from there one day, he was

57

able to prevent the execution of a Turkish girl caught while making love. By order of the Waiwode (or Governor) of Athens she had been sewn into a sack and was about to be thrown into the sea. Bribery, effective where threats produced mere sullenness, saved the girl and Byron sent her away to Thebes. There is a suggestion that he perhaps knew the girl better than he admitted; in any case, he used the incident in his later poem, *The Giaour*, and it is clear that, possibly because it had allowed him direct action, opportunities for which he never avoided, it made a considerable impression on him.

By September, travelling once more, with Nicolo in his company, he had fallen ill; 'I have been vomited and purged according to rule,' he wrote to Hobhouse, adding a week later that he had been 'five days bed-ridden with Emetics, glysters, Bark, and all the host of Physic'. Nicolo, too, had caught the fever, but by the end of the year both were back in Athens again, Byron sociable, happy to spend time with temporarily established foreigners; as he wrote to Hobhouse in January, there were many English visitors in the city, 'with all of whom I have been and *am* on dining terms, and we have had balls and a variety of fooleries with the females of Athens'. But at the same time he was, in essays based on what he had written of Greece in *Childe Harold's Pilgrimage*, setting out his ideas about Greek nationalism and the struggle for liberty: 'the interposition of foreigners alone can emancipate the Greeks. . . .'

By now, Byron's energy, his earlier need for travel, seems to have somewhat drained away. He was given permission to travel in Syria and Egypt, both still a part of the Ottoman Empire, but in the end did not set out on the journey. His foreign friends who had made the Athens winter agreeably wild began to leave; he gave a farewell dinner for some of them. He fell ill, with minor disabilities this time – 'a cough and a catarrh and the piles'. It was time to go home. Yet he seems also to have hoped for nothing from England and, although he was still writing, had told his mother that 'scribbling' was 'a disease I hope myself cured of'. His shortage of money would hardly be altered by his return; on the contrary, he could live far more cheaply in Greece. Nevertheless, in April 1811, Byron left Piraeus in the *Hydra*, the lamentations of his servants ringing in his ears, bound for Malta on the first stage of the journey home.

In Malta he had two painful farewells to survive; one with Mrs Spencer Smith, a belated leave-taking with a woman who had, quite probably, kept the possibility of his loving return before her for two years as someone in the dark might hoard a candle; the other with Nicolo, whom he was putting into a school in Malta. The boy seems certainly to have been at least as steadfast as Mrs Spencer Smith, for he wrote to an increasingly indifferent Byron for several years. Byron, who had allowed him £7000 in the will he drew up on his return to England, ignored him in the one of 1815. In any case, on Malta in 1811, all this emotion, alternating as it did with Byron's recurrent fever, left him both physically and mentally very low: 'neither my health nor my hitherto hoydenish spirits are as rampant as usual,' he wrote to Hobhouse from the *Volage*, the frigate which was carrying him back to England. He arrived at Sheerness on 14 June, expecting little, uncertain of his future, insecure financially, largely unknown. It is likely that, despite all his protestations, it was this last disability which irked him most and which he would most have liked to reverse.

An illustration from Childe
Harold.

3 Fame

But who can view the ripen'd rose, nor seek
To wear it? who can curiously behold
The smoothness and the sheen of beauty's cheek,
Nor feel the heart can never all grow old?
Who can contemplate Fame through clouds unfold
The star which rises o'er her steep, nor climb?

DURING HIS RETURN TO ENGLAND, Byron had considered his life, his mood veering between the gloomy and the anguished as he made a list of why changes were needed. The list began, 'At twenty-three the best of life is over and its bitters double. 2ndly I have seen mankind in various Countries and find them equally despicable. . . .' He goes on to mention his lameness, which would, he thought, 'render his old age more peevish & intolerable', his growing selfishness and misanthropy, the state of his affairs, which were 'gloomy enough'. He ends this recital with '7thly I have outlived all my appetites and most of my vanities, aye even the vanity of authorship'. It was therefore in something of a desperate state of mind that he came back to London; he had been for two years free of the implicit demands his own environment made on him, free to become whatever he pleased in a society which had few preconceptions about what he should be. He had been a foreigner in Greece, and thus truly alienated from his surroundings, not at all answerable for his conduct and beliefs in the way a native must be.

Yet for a moment it seemed as though everything would continue as it had before. There was Scrope Davies at his doorstep, drunken and witty as ever. There was Dallas, a bore but a distant kinsman, a sort of unctuous toady to whom, with a generosity which continued as everything else did, Byron gave the copyright of *Childe Harold's Pilgrimage*. As a consequence, there were negotiations with John Murray, the second in a long line of (still-continuing) publishers, who was to become Byron's friend, bringing out with a sturdiness not perhaps absolute yet surprising in one of his profession, much of the poet's most controversial and scandalising work. There were finances to see to, and there was Hanson to consult. There were eager greetings from Hobhouse, now a captain in the militia at Dover. And then, abruptly, death intervened.

On 1 August he heard that his mother was seriously ill. He was trying to raise money for the journey to Newstead when a second message told him of her death. At Newstead, he sat by her body, bursting into tears induced, one cannot help feeling, more by the occasion than true feeling; 'Oh, Mrs By,' he said to her old maid, 'I had but one friend in the world, and she is gone.' But without time for recovery, a second blow fell: Skinner Matthews, brilliant, a daring intellectual, as witty a sensualist as Byron himself, died, trapped by weeds, drowned in the Cam he and Byron had swum in so often. Byron wrote to Scrope Davies, 'Some curse hangs over

PREVIOUS PAGES LEFT Lady Caroline Lamb, by Thomas Phillips.
RIGHT Annabella Milbanke about the time of her first meeting with Byron, when she was twenty. By George Hayter.

OPPOSITE John Murray II
To thee, with hope and
terror dumb
The unfledged MS. authors
come;
Thou printest all – and
sellest some – My Murray.

64

London in the early nineteenth century. St James's Street, with Boodles Club on the left and Brook Club opposite.

me and mine. My mother lies a corpse in this house; one of my best friends is drowned in a ditch.' But the catalogue of mortality was not yet over; within a few days Byron heard that a Harrow friend, John Wingfield, had also died. All three had, he wrote to Hobhouse, 'disappeared in one little month, since *my return*, and without my seeing *either*, though I have *heard* from *all*. . . . There is to me something so incomprehensible about death, that I can neither speak nor think on the subject. Indeed, when I looked on the mass of corruption which was the being from whence I sprung, I doubted within myself whether I *was*, or she *was not*. I have lost her who gave me being, and some of those who made that being a blessing.'

It was now that he sat down and made the will in which the distant Nicolo was left £7000. But life summoned, after all; Murray wanted to bring out *Childe Harold*, but not anonymously. Byron, always less disdainful of the world's opinion than his later poses have allowed us to believe, did not care to be scarred another time by the critics, nor to be identified so closely with the poem's moody hero. He expected trouble; several of his friends were particularly eager to have him alter lines which expressed his scepticism, his almost free-thinking unconcern for the susceptibilities of convinced Christians. Byron was firm: 'I will have nothing to do with your immortality; we are miserable enough in this life, without the absurdity of speculating upon another. . . . As to revealed religion, Christ came to save men; but a good Pagan will go to heaven, and a bad Nazarene to hell . . . who will believe that God will damn men for not knowing what they were never taught?' Thus he rebutted the earnest arguments of Francis Hodgson, resident tutor at King's College, Cambridge, one of the friends he had made while at the University. He added that while he had been 'on a bed of sickness in a far-distant country' he had 'looked to death as a relief from pain, without a wish for an after-life, but a confidence that the God who punishes in this existence had left that last asylum for the weary'.

Death had not yet done with him, however, for it was now that he learned that Edleston, too, had died, the previous May. It was October; Byron wrote to Dallas: 'My friends fall around me, and I shall be left a lonely tree before I am withered.' The sense of doom that so often possessed him, the feeling that he was the particularly damned of a damned family, must have been strong in him at this time. He wrote to Hobhouse, 'now though I should never have seen him again (and it is very proper that I should not) I have been

67

more affected than I should care to own elsewhere'. It was now that he wrote the stanzas of *Childe Harold* lamenting youth, the passing of love, the death of the unnamed, but haunting, Edleston:

Thou too art gone, thou loved and lovely one!
Whom Youth and Youth's affections bound to me. . .
All thou couldst have of mine, stern Death! thou hast;
The Parent, Friend, and now the more than friend. . .

But the future had its own demands to make; he began to be known in the literary circles of London – he met Rogers and Campbell, and particularly Thomas Moore, who having once challenged Byron (there had been references to an earlier absurd, but would-be-bloody, encounter with Jeffrey, editor of the *Edinburgh Review*, in *English Bards, and Scotch Reviewers*), now half-heartedly challenged again, but was easily mollified. In this slightly ridiculous manner Byron made the acquaintance of a man whose poems he had read with delight as a boy, whom he still respected, and who was to remain his lifelong friend.

Christmas 1812 he spent at Newstead, with Hodgson as his guest, and Harness, a boy he had protected at Harrow, perhaps because he, too, was lame. The evenings now were very different from the monk-robed rioting which had scandalised the neighbourhood three years earlier, although Byron, not one to accept celibacy without a struggle, had introduced new maids to play mistress under his roof, particularly a Welsh girl named Susan who turned out to be more lively than loyal. As always, being deceived brought to the surface Byron's self-pity, that bittersweet savouring of a pain which could never be assuaged, and which, while genuine, was yet in some manner contrived. To Hodgson he derided his 'vanity in fancying that such a thing as I am could ever be beloved'.

But other excitements now involved him. In February, he made his maiden speech in the House of Lords, for a while reviving in that effort all the old oratorical ambitions of his youth. His manner may have been, as he himself thought, 'a little theatrical', but his object, to oppose a bill making death the penalty for framebreaking, was serious enough. Recently devised machines had been putting weavers out of work, as their hitherto fragmented industry was rationalised and the great mills were built. In retaliation, they had smashed the new weaving frames, soldiers had been brought in to curb them and riots had resulted. Byron insisted that 'nothing but absolute want could have driven a

OPPOSITE 'Gentleman' John Jackson, the famous pugilist, gave Byron boxing lessons and became a good friend of his. His portrait used to hang in Byron's rooms at Cambridge and is now in his bedroom at Newstead Abbey.

large, and once honest and industrious, body of people into the commission of excesses so hazardous. . . . How will you carry the Bill into effect? Can you commit a whole country to their own prisons? Will you erect a gibbet in every field, and hang up men like scarecrows?'

The general feeling was that the speech had been impressive; Byron was appointed to a committee which amended the bill by removing the death penalty – although the House of Commons later restored it. But Byron's position in politics was a little anomalous. He was by instinct a Radical, yet had an aristocrat's disdain of Radicals. For the main body of Whigs, however, he was too extreme. He soon realised that Parliament with its protocol and its hypocrisy would never do for him. As it was, *Childe Harold* opened another route for him.

Byron, maimed in childhood both in body and spirit, was a life-long glutton for love, for friendship, for acceptance. It was as though he existed only before mirrors; their reflections confirmed him. He forced the world's recognition as though without it he could not know he was there. In a sense, he had to, for if the world's awareness of him had not been constantly renewed and reinforced, he would have been thrown back upon what he always suspected – that he was not worthy to be loved. On 10 March Murray published *Childe Harold's Pilgrimage*, and the world's awareness rushed upon him. 'I awoke one morning and found myself famous,' as he put it.

It was not only as a poet that he was now so widely known, it was as the embodiment of his own hero, this

> shameless wight
> Sore given to revel, and ungodly glee;
> Few earthly things found savour in his sight
> Save concubines and carnal companie. . .

He had run through 'Sin's long labyrinth' and had 'sighed to many though he loved but one' who 'alas! could ne'er be his'. It is clear that this mixture of gothic guilt and tragic rejection became lethal to women when embodied in the pale, slim (the diets continued), curly headed, blue-eyed figure of his slightly limping lordship. This caused some problems; Lady Falkland, for example, whose husband had been killed in a duel and to whom in the most gentle manner Byron had once given £500, a sum he could not afford, decided that he had long been secretly in love with her. An extended series of letters, to which he made no answer,

OPPOSITE Byron as Childe Harold, the epitome of the Byronic Hero.
In my youth's summer I did sing of One,
The wandering outlaw of his own dark mind . . .

71

ran the gamut from happy acceptance to noble rejection, a one-sided dialogue with a Byron who existed only in her imagination.

A true dialogue was, however, about to begin. At Lady Westmoreland's, surrounded by the gush and clamour of a clutch of lion-hunting ladies, he saw abruptly turning away from him a slim, fair-haired young woman, with dark, hazel eyes in a heart-shaped face. Her rejection of him made her more memorable than all the simpering beauties signalling their availability around him. He was not to know that she had already written to him anonymously – 'You deserve to be and you shall be happy. Do not throw away such Talents as you possess in gloom & regrets for the past. . . .' – nor that in her private journal she was to describe him as 'mad – bad – and dangerous to know'.

Lady Caroline Lamb was twenty-seven, impulsive, vivacious, energetic, perhaps almost neurotically so, a young woman thrusting at the limits of even those lax conventions which the libertine Regency had left people of her class, outspoken, almost shocking, given to dressing in the uniforms of pages and to uttering opinions which left the more orthodox trembling. She was married to William Lamb, the second son of Lord and Lady Melbourne, a curiously cool man, despite moments of instability, almost happy, one feels, to observe his wife's increasing passion for this fascinating, fashionable poet, loving her, yet not possessive, accepting her vagaries and extravagancies of temperament for as long as anyone could be expected to; already, it seems, one can discern the wisdom and courtesy he was to show when, as Lord Melbourne and Prime Minister, he became the young Queen Victoria's first political mentor. He and his wife lived in a suite of rooms at Melbourne House. Although they often quarrelled – it was hard to avoid quarrelling with Caroline, who had always had an appalling temper – he was not overly concerned with morality; 'I might flirt and go about with whom I pleased,' she reported later. Adultery, of course, was more the norm than the exception at their social level: Lamb himself was almost certainly the son of Lord Egremont, rather than of Melbourne, and his younger brother George – the offspring, it was rumoured, of the Prince of Wales – married the Duchess of Devonshire's illegitimate daughter. Byron, fascinated, soon became a constant visitor at Melbourne House, but, although already captivated by Caroline Lamb – his 'Caro' – he nevertheless found a moment to notice on his second visit 'a young lady, more simply dressed than the rest of the assembly, sitting alone upon

72

a sofa'. The young lady's name was Annabella Milbanke, she was William Lamb's cousin, and it may have been better if she had not been there, or if Byron had not noticed her, either then or ever. (He had stumbled on his way into the house – a bad omen, he was later to think.)

Caroline Lamb had her own circle, and was known for her almost eccentric unconcern for the opinions of others, and Byron, whose frozen-faced arrogance and vocabulary of sarcasm covered profound insecurities, may well have been nervous of her at first. 'Your Ladyship, I am told, likes all that is new and rare for a moment,' he said to her, offering her a rose and a carnation; it was hard for him to believe that she might be serious about him, for he was unused to dealing on level terms with the passions of his equals. Within a month of their meeting, however, they had become lovers – although Byron remained the wonder of Society and the glory of the Season. And among those who, still from a distance, followed his progress with a kind of condescending fascination, was Annabella Milbanke: her curiosity, she had written to her mother in March, had been 'much gratified' by seeing Lord Byron – 'It is said that he is an infidel, and I think it probable from the general character of his mind.' One can tell how her thoughts were already running from a diary entry of about this time, in which she set down her conviction 'that he is sincerely repentant for the evil he has done, though he has not the resolution (without aid) to adopt a new course of conduct. . . .' The self-revelation of that 'without aid', imbued as it is with the feminine certainty that 'bad' men are redeemable, if only they are given guidance, was to have sad consequences. Byron, a man concerned to heal his wounds with the affection of the world, though in the long run always on his own terms, may well have sensed her need to see him wavering on the bleak edge of redemption; and, as Marchand puts it, he had 'an uncanny capacity for displaying that part of his personality which would most engage the person with whom he was talking'.

Annabella sent her own poems to Byron (by way of Caroline) and Caroline became a little jealous of the attention he paid her. Almost unnecessarily frank, Byron replied to 'My Dear Lady Caroline' that the poems displayed 'fancy, feeling, and . . . facility of expression. . . . She certainly is a very extraordinary girl; who would imagine so much strength and variety of thought under that placid Countenance?' Nevertheless, it was Caro who now stood unchallenged at the centre of his life. During the long, self-

OPPOSITE Lady Caroline Lamb: 'You know I have always thought you the cleverest, most agreeable, absurd, amiable, perplexing, dangerous, fascinating little being that lives now, or ought to have lived 2000 years ago.'

75

indulgent evenings in the great houses of London, he came to understand, possibly for the first time, the acid power of jealousy. The waltz had just come into fashion; debarred from dancing it himself, he could not stand to see her dance it with others. He asked Caroline to give the dance up; she, who delighted in it, obeyed. He grew jealous of William Lamb, a tall, handsome, graceful man; when she would not swear instantly that she loved him better than her husband, Byron would threaten, 'I'll wring that little obstinate heart.' And of course he did. It may be that Caroline, used to the fantasticated, half-imagined *amours* of her circle, thought that Byron would be just another conquest, a milestone to mark yet one more London season. But Byron, hungry for the love of others as a vampire for blood, was not to be dealt with so lightly. If his fangs struck – and they never struck unless he too was deeply moved – he drained his victims of their very life. Later, Caroline was to write to him. 'When first you told me in the Carriage to kiss your mouth & I durst not – & after thinking it such

Holland House, the Kensington mansion of Lord Holland, was the centre of fashionable aristocratic and literary London.

76

William Lamb, the future
Lord Melbourne and
husband of Caroline.

a crime it was more than I could prevent from that moment – you drew me to you like a magnet & I could not indeed I could not have kept away. . . .'

The affair blazed like a fire, and London regarded its brilliance with awe – and some malice. It was all too open, too fierce; the conventions were not being observed, feeling had overturned reticence. No one objected to adultery, pleasure, the sound of acquiescent laughter from behind closed doors, but decency demanded that love should be surrounded by a sort of public secrecy in which no one was excluded from the truth, although no one admitted it was known. But, as Caro said, 'I run and gallop and drive as if for a wager' – she could do nothing slowly, nothing stealthily or deviously; she had never learned to care about the opinions of those about her. It was to be, in a sense, her tragedy, for when Byron, his volatile feelings burned out after two months, began to turn from her, she could not accept it; indeed, in a sense she never did accept it. She had lived through the most crucial experience of her life, and nothing in it would ever be the same again.

Byron, with Hobhouse and his cousin and heir, Captain George Byron, travelled to Newstead for what Hobhouse called a 'delirium of sensuality'. He met Lady Oxford, an older, subtler, perhaps more intelligent woman soon to stand in Caroline's place – though it was a somewhat cooler place with her in it. Caroline, meanwhile, would not believe that passion was over. She bombarded Byron with letters, appeared in the places and houses he did. As she wrote to him, self-aware but beyond self-help, 'I expose myself to every eye, to every unkind observation.' She visited Byron, disguised – with under the disguise one of her favourite page's outfits. She threatened to stab herself; Byron had to prevent her and Hobhouse, who was there, finally took her to a friend's house. In early August she sent him a present – tendrils of her pubic hair. 'I cut the hair too close & bled much more than you need – do not you do the same. . . .' The gift had an inscription which began, 'Caroline Byron – next to Thyrsa dearest & most faithful. . . .' Byron had used the name Thyrsa to disguise the sex and identity of Edleston in the poems he had written after the young man's death; it is likely therefore that Caroline knew of his love for Edleston and perhaps for other youths, especially since Byron's passion for Nicolo (still faithfully writing from Malta) had been his last before succumbing to Caro.

Caroline was not yet finished. She ran away for a while – 'I am apprehensive for her personal safety, for her state of mind,' Byron wrote to Lady Melbourne. 'Here I sit alone, and however I might *appear* to you, in the most painful suspense.' It was he who eventually found her and sent her home to her husband and his family. In September, William Lamb took her to Ireland. Byron wrote her a farewell, although his authorship of the letter has been disputed. Perhaps Caroline forged it, as she certainly did other notes, notably to Murray, yet he seems to have been quite capable of its tone of maudlin formality. His letter to Annabella Milbanke after her acceptance of his proposal bears witness to this, as in another way do his letters to her after her departure. His words to Caroline judicially mixed tenderness with resignation:

If tears which you saw and know I am not apt to shed . . . have not sufficiently proved what my real feelings are, and must ever be towards you, my love, I have no other proof to offer. God knows, I wish you happy, and when I quit you, or rather you, from a sense of duty to your husband and mother, quit me, you shall acknowledge the truth of what

I again promise and vow, that no other in word or deed, shall ever hold the place in my affections, which is, and shall be, most sacred to you, till I am nothing. . . . I shall have a pride, a melancholy pleasure, in suffering what you yourself can scarcely conceive. . . .

The words pick their way carefully through the appearances of feeling, as though the only use of phrases was pretence. But then, abruptly, comes a postscript, and one feels Byron's conscience would not allow him to offer Caroline so shabby a vocabulary, that his emotions had after all to break through in all their own genuine power; he asks her if there is anything 'on earth or heaven that would have made me so happy as to have made you mine long ago? And not less *now* than *then*, but *more* than ever at

Lady Caroline Lamb. 'I was and am yours freely and most entirely,' wrote Byron in August 1812, 'to obey, to honour, love, – and fly with you when, where and how you yourself *might* and *may* determine.'

this time. . . . I was and am yours freely and most entirely, to obey, to honour, love, – and fly with you when, where and how you yourself *might* and *may* determine.' Byron's most extreme vice, perhaps, was his need to feel that he was feeling; he pressed emotions to appear, and when they did so, over-indulged them. It is as if he were only properly alive when sentiment – and senti- mentality – animated him. It is no wonder that poor Caroline, faced with this mixture of the lukewarm and the lava-hot, should continue to believe he loved her.

Byron, buoyed up by the thought that Newstead, sold at last, was to bring him £140,000 (in the event, the buyer would pre- varicate about the payment almost beyond Byron's – and Hanson's – endurance, before finally withdrawing), went to Cheltenham to regain a measure of calm. For posterity, and perhaps for him, the one consequence of real value to his relationship with Lady Caroline Lamb was the friendship which resulted from it with her mother-in-law, Lady Melbourne. As the varied paternity of her children suggests, Lady Melbourne had a flexible attitude to conventional morality and from this time onwards Byron used her as in some ways his most intimate confidante. He needed an audience, and one of sufficient wit and liveliness to follow, and delight in, his own cynical adroitness on the page. It is likely that his affairs, and the attitudes he struck, titillated her and that in a way, involved in this vicarious sexuality, she acted out, at one remove, what even a few of her more perceptive contemporaries saw as a kind of infatuation for him. As for him, he confessed that 'with a little more youth, Lady M. might have turned my head'.

His head, however, was now not so much turned as confused, haunted still by the clamorous ghost of Caroline Lamb. He stilled it, rigorously: 'I was, am, and shall be, I fear,' he wrote to Lady Melbourne, 'attached to another, one to whom I have never said much, but have never lost sight of. . . . As I have said so much, I may as well say all. The woman I mean is Miss Milbanke. . . .' Yet in letter after letter he nags at his feelings for Caroline, is gloomy about their prospects should they continue, fatalistic about that continuance if Caroline wished for it: 'For my part, it is an accursed business, *towards* nor *from* which I shall not move a single step. . . . As to Annabella, she requires time and all the cardinal virtues, and in the interim I am a little verging towards one who demands neither, and saves me besides the trouble of marrying, by being married already.' He was discovering comfort of a sort in the charms of an Italian singer.

OPPOSITE Lady Melbourne, Caroline Lamb's mother-in- law, later became Byron's confidante. 'I look upon you as my good genius,' he wrote to her after his affair with Caroline had come to an end.

81

After a little sounding-out, Lady Melbourne told Annabella Milbanke of Byron's proposal. Annabella was after all her brother's daughter, and Byron had already half-jokingly suggested that she should make the approach, 'were it only for the pleasure of calling you *aunt*!' Annabella, after some rather arid cogitation, turned the offer down. She wrote, perhaps to order her own thoughts, a pen picture of Byron – it mentioned 'the uncorrupted purity of his moral sense' and ended abruptly in the middle of what might have been a piece of wish-fulfillment: 'He is extremely humble towards persons whose character he respects, and to them he would probably confess his errors. . . .' Byron, sent a version of this by Lady Melbourne, commented that it was 'more favourable to her talents than her discernment' and dubbed her, partly because of her skill in mathematics, his 'Princess of Parallelograms' – 'Her proceedings are quite rectangular, or rather we are two parallel lines prolonged to infinity side by side, but never to meet.'

Happily, perhaps, he wandered off into a new, attractive pasture. Lady Oxford had invited him to her country house, Eywood, and it was now that he became her lover. One suspects that what he called 'love' was rarely more than the intense interaction of sexual desire dressed up in the vocabulary of a more permanent emotion, to dignify both it and himself. He understood very well that these feelings were short-term and scoffed at the idea that they might be longer-lasting – yet used the phrases of constancy as if, cynical though he was, and honest as he always remained, he nevertheless wished to deceive himself.

In any case, he was 'in love' now with Lady Oxford, mature, practised, and providing, after the Carolingian storms, a lulling haven. Yet Caroline could penetrate even here; she was a friend of Lady Oxford's and so, hearing rumours of Byron's involvement with another, wrote and asked her to intercede. But when she discovered that it was Lady Oxford, her 'dearest Aspasia', who had taken her place, her fury and despair were, as always, intemperate. She threatened suicide. She repented having allowed herself to be brought back after her disappearance: 'Oh that I had not been weak enough to return when Lord Byron brought me back, that I had never returned. . . . Lord Byron has *now* sealed my destruction, and it shall follow. . . .' Byron's response to all this was cool; to Lady Melbourne he described Caroline's letter as 'foolish' and 'headstrong' – 'She has hurt and disgusted me by her latter conduct beyond expression, and even if I did not love

another, I would never speak to her again. . . . This *was* to be broken off – it is broken off.' He could not, he added, 'exist without some object of love. I have found one with whom I am perfectly satisfied, and who as far as I can judge is no less so with me; our mutual wish is *quiet*. . . .'

On the same day, Byron also wrote to Caroline, his tone terse, even contemptuous:

Our affections are not in our power – mine are engaged. I love another – were I inclined to reproach you, I might for 20 thousand things, but I will not. . . . My opinion of you is entirely alter'd, & if I had wanted anything to confirm me, your Levities, your caprices, & the mean subterfuges you have lately made use of while madly gay . . . would entirely have open'd my eyes. I am no longer your lover. . . .

Byron, having promised Lady Oxford – and it must have been easy to do so – that he would not meet Caroline, remained contentedly at Eywood. Annabella receded from his mind; the contemplated marriage, he now felt, had been happily escaped: 'That would have been but a *cold collation*, and I prefer hot suppers.' Caroline, meanwhile, vengeful if distant, burnt Byron in effigy.

Yet London beckoned, and the Season, and Lady Oxford's exalted friend, the Princess of Wales. Serenity was disturbed, partly by Lady Oxford's half-habitual interest in other handsome young men-about-Society, partly by Byron's wilfulness and, if his wife's later testimony is to be believed, because he attempted to seduce Lady Oxford's thirteen-year-old daughter. At the same time, the Newstead sale was hanging fire, and the House of Lords, which he attended now and again, had begun to bore him. To cap all this, Lady Caroline returned to town, as militant as ever. He contemplated escape, revolving three possibilities of travel. Caroline asked for a lock of his hair in remembrance; with fairly black humour, he sent her some strands of Lady Oxford's, before returning more moodily than ever before to Eywood. Yet here too Caroline's letters pursued him and when he was next in London he at last consented to meet her. While Byron has left no record of what took place then, Caroline said later: 'he asked me to forgive him; he looked sorry for me; he cried.' This is very likely, for Byron was addicted to the immediate emotions – he loved and laughed and wept with great intensity, yet rarely for long. It is understandable if Caroline felt that he still had some held-back residue of his former love for her, that she still had some chance of drawing him back to her. And so she might have, had the matter

OPPOSITE Byron at twenty-five, 'mad, bad and dangerous to know'.

85

lain between her and him, but there were too many others in the circus – Lady Oxford, who returned to London late in May, Annabella Milbanke, whom he met once more, to her unexpected agitation, Lady Melbourne, who sat in her epistolary observation-post like some amoral and lubricious goddess regarding the undisciplined antics of mortals.

Byron made his last speech in the House of Lords, in support of the extreme Radical, Cartwright, whose petition to reform Parliament had been unlawfully obstructed by the Government. As a result of his stand, Byron knocked out from under himself every last plank of moderate support he might have hoped for and so ended his chance of a political career. Almost despite himself, it was as a writer that he would now continue to build his reputation – as a writer who presented himself as hero, who in the world's estimation lived his own poems, who wrapped himself perhaps more inextricably than anyone ever had before him in the coils and moods and attitudes of his own verse. He was working now on *The Giaour*, a poem based to some extent on his adventures in the Levant and including an account of his rescue of the Turkish girl condemned to death for her sexual indiscretions. Lady Oxford abruptly departed, on travels which it was at one time intended he should share – 'I feel more *Carolinish* about her than I expected,' he confessed to Lady Melbourne. But in the drawing-rooms of the mighty he now appeared occasionally with a new companion – his half-sister, Augusta.

There was both the comfort of the familiar and the piquancy of the strange about her. They had hardly been together since their earliest childhood, although they had corresponded, and they had not met since Byron's return from Greece. She had something of his profile, something of his luminous eyes, something of his mobile, expressive mouth, but all softened, toned-down, more rounded, gentler – in a word, more feminine. She understood him and, although five years older than he, responded to his humour with an ease which must have delighted him, happy as he always was with a receptive audience. She knew the circumstances of his childhood, she understood the sources of his pride and his uncertainty. In a sense, his Childe Harold moodiness, his public face, supercilious, cold, often half-sneering, even his wit and conviviality when he unbent, did not deceive her; she knew him. Pretence was unavailing with her, but revelation unnecessary. Having known him early, she took her knowledge for granted. It seems likely, indeed, that she always knew him better than he did

OPPOSITE Augusta Leigh.
We were and are – I am,
even as thou art –
Beings who ne'er each
other can resign . . .

86

Thomas Moore, Byron's friend and confidant. Byron often teased him affectionately both in letters and verse.
What are you doing now,
  Oh Thomas Moore?
Sighing or suing now,
Rhyming or wooing now,
Billing or cooing now,
  Which, Thomas Moore?

her, although she may never have codified her understanding. Yet, despite this underlying closeness, she was physically a stranger to him, a person he had not seen since he was a boy. And he was for her something of a figure to reverence, this highly successful poet, this man who wandered, known and even courted, about the fashionable labyrinths of Society.

Yet Caroline Lamb was not to be discarded so easily. There was an incident at Lady Heathcote's: did she, as *The Satirist* asserted, take up 'as pretty a little dessert-knife as a Lady could desire to commit suicide with', and stab herself? Was she, as she said much later, made furious by being at last given Byron's permission to waltz, the lifting of a prohibition which, though she suffered from it, must have seemed to her satisfying proof of his continuing jealousy? 'I clasped the knife, not intending anything. "Do, my dear," he said, "if you mean to act a Roman's part, mind which way you strike with your knife – be it at your own heart, not mine – you have struck there already. . . .'" But she had not struck herself, she said; instead, the knife was pulled out of her hand by others, crowding round, 'my hand got cut, & the blood came over

88

my gown. . . .' But then she told Tom Moore that a bottle had broken and her cut had been an accident. Her mother-in-law agreed it was broken glass which had made the wound, but said that Caroline had deepened it with a pair of scissors. In any case, the incident was a scandal. Rumour could not be helped, gossip was a positive pleasure, but open display of deep feeling was vulgar and not to be borne. Good taste, though hard to define, was nevertheless easy to understand – it was perhaps Caroline Lamb's misfortune that she had never understood it. 'She is now like a Barrel of Gunpowder,' Lady Melbourne wrote gloomily. But she always had been. Indeed, one sometimes has the feeling that it was precisely this lack of moderation which most made Byron uneasy, not simply because it made her so hard to put up with, but because it showed up his own careful awareness of where the limits of permissible behaviour lay. When he shocked the watching world, it was with a nice appreciation of what it could stand and of what was due to a man in his position. The only criticism which did not hurt him was that which he had deliberately provoked; it was to provoke it that he wore his masks.

Caroline Lamb, on the other hand, did as she pleased. She had no need to demand or even demonstrate her personal liberty, for she always assumed she had it. When she loved, love ruled her, and when she was turned away, despair brought her to violence, hysteria and, possibly, madness. There never was a person less addicted to masks than she.

But by August, Byron was, as he wrote to Tom Moore, 'in a far more serious, and entirely new, scrape than any of the past twelve months – and that is saying a good deal'. It seems clear, although there is no direct evidence for it, that this 'new scrape' was his sexual relation with Augusta Leigh, his half-sister – adultery and incest in one. Certainly it was in this direction that his thoughts were tending, for it was in 1813 that he wrote *The Bride of Abydos*, the story of a love between a brother and sister – although in the end it turns out, perhaps to avoid shocking an inflammable public, to be no more than the permissible passion felt for each other by cousins. It is probable that greater even than the somehow comfortable love which he felt for Augusta was Byron's conviction that he and all those who shared his blood were doomed to perform acts of the darkest wickedness, that there was a curse upon the family. Yet he could not resist his interest straying elsewhere, most notably in the direction of Lady Frances Webster, whose husband was either a fatuously complacent fool or a

OVERLEAF Illustration from
The Bride of Abydos.
Beneath the garden's
wicket porch
Far flash'd on high a
blazing torch!
Another – and another –
and another –
'Oh fly – no more – yet
now my more than brother!'

devious lecher determined for his own purposes to have Byron debauch his wife: in fairness, it must be said that contemporary opinion inclines to the former verdict. He repeatedly told Byron that his wife was above suspicion – and that as a result he felt all other women fair game; he congratulated himself on possessing a wife 'without passion' who was safe from other men; at the same time, he tended to display a short-tempered jealousy without being given much cause. Byron was not a man to resist such an implicit challenge, particularly when, by the interchange of secret notes, it became clear that the lady was not as indifferent to desire as he had been led to suppose. Alone with him at Newstead, she told him, 'I am entirely at your mercy. . . . Now act as you will.' But her speech, full of prophecies of the remorse she would feel if he proceeded – 'I cannot bear the reflection hereafter' – cooled his determination. He wrote to Lady Melbourne, 'Was I wrong? I spared her. . . .'

This scene, played out at two in the morning, proved to be the high point of the unconsummated passion between them; once returned to London, there were other concerns to engross him, other women to pursue. Augusta still preoccupied him – and, like a practised gambler hedging his bets, he kept up an intermittent correspondence with Miss Milbanke, who was now hinting that her reason for refusing him was a prior suitor (there had been some but this one was a fiction). Letters still passed to and fro between him and Caroline Lamb, although they avoided meeting. Yet in the journal he began that November of 1813, he displays a perhaps slightly studied self-disgust – 'At five-and-twenty, when the better part of life is over, one should be *something*; – and what am I? nothing but five-and-twenty. . . .' He wanted to get married and it sometimes seems as though it hardly mattered to him who his wife might be. It was a mythical stability he hankered after – committed to marriage in this way, he might even have been turned into a husband by a more accommodating woman than the one he chose. But on the last day of November he was writing of Annabella Milbanke: 'What an odd situation and friendship is ours! – without one spark of love on either side. . . .'; nevertheless she was 'a very superior woman, and very little spoiled, which is strange in an heiress. . . . Any other head would be turned with half her acquisitions, and a tenth of her advantages.' The next day, as though to answer an unspoken proposition, he was writing of his cousin, George Byron, 'I hope he will be an admiral, and, perhaps, Lord Byron into the bargain. If he would but marry, I would engage never to marry myself. . . . He would be happier, and I should like nephews better than sons.' For the moment, in any case, Augusta, humorous, docile and undemanding, kept him from precipitate action. He groaned in Calvinistic self-disgust, yet sank into the comforts of affection and, who knows, reciprocal desire.

The year turned, and Byron's twenty-sixth birthday loomed. He watched *The Bride of Abydos* disappear from the booksellers' shelves, worked on *The Corsair*, fretted at passing time, passing youth: 'Is there anything in the future that can possibly console us for not being always *twenty-five*?' Lady Frances mooned, disconsolate and, one suspects, frustrated, still unseduced by the great seducer – 'A few kisses, for which she was no worse, and I no better,' as he described the affair to Lady Melbourne. And, a revenant from his childhood, Mary Chaworth, suddenly sidled into his life in a series of coy letters and invitations, signs of regret, perhaps, at not noticing in the lumpy Harrovian of ten years earlier the devilish genius the world now acclaimed. Byron, stirred, half-tempted, managed nevertheless to keep his distance; Mrs Musters, the one-time Miss Chaworth, persisted for a while, complaining of her husband, her health, her lot. Byron, bewildered, wrote to Lady Melbourne, 'I do believe that to marry would be my wisest step – but whom? . . . But all wives would be much the same. I have no *heart* to spare and expect none in return. . . .' Whoever he married, he said, 'might do as she pleased, so that she had a fair temper, and a *quiet* way of conducting herself, leaving me the same liberty of conscience. What I want is a companion – a friend rather than a sentimentalist. I have seen enough of love matches. . . .'

Byron retired to Newstead with Augusta, now pregnant; he was happy to be marooned there by the snow, content with his companion – they laughed, he said, 'much more than is suitable to so solid a mansion'. In London, John Murray added another layer to the Byronic mask when he published *The Corsair*. People struggled to buy their copies and on the first day of publication ten thousand copies were sold, 'a thing perfectly unprecedented', Murray pointed out excitedly to Byron. By mid-February, Byron was in London again. A month later, with Augusta now eight months pregnant, Annabella marked a revival in her fortunes by inviting him to meet her parents. 'I shall be in love with her again if I don't care,' Byron sentimentally informed himself in his journal.

Byron's bedroom at Newstead Abbey. The bed is the one Byron had in his rooms at Cambridge and the portraits of Joe Murray and 'Gentleman' John Jackson still hang on the walls.

And at the same time, he found himself distressed by the fate of his hero, Napoleon, the undisputed Great Man of the age, the self-willed, self-created, totally untrammelled conqueror, who stood for freedom whatever his tyrannies, who took what his will demanded and made the hierarchies of Europe buckle under his assault. It was the ignominious manner of his surrender which most disturbed Byron: 'What! wait till they were in his capital, and then talk of his readiness to give up what is already gone! . . . I am utterly bewildered and confounded.'

It was at about this time that he learned of the birth, on 15 April, of Augusta's daughter, Medora. Was Byron really her father? It seems very probable, and she herself was led to believe so – but then any woman might prefer an illustrious poet for a father instead of a nonentity, given the opportunity to choose. Byron seems neither to have acknowledged her nor to have picked her out in any way from Augusta's other children, which contrasts with his concern for his other two known daughters. But would he have demonstrated Medora's especial importance for him and thus risked his sister's reputation? So, while one must assume, if only from the months Augusta spent with him, that the child was his, to some degree the puzzle still remains.

Uncertain as to his feelings about Annabella, he seems to have allowed silence to cover indecision; in May, she wondered why he had not written, in June, she begged for a reply. But Byron, by then hectically involved in fashionable London's post-war euphoria, had better things to do than pursue this indecisive correspondence with a primly uncertain, self-consciously puritanical amateur mathematician. In July, he journeyed to Hastings with Augusta, instead of to Seaham to visit Annabella. Augusta, however, was urging him to find a wife – 'She wished me much to marry,' he confided later to Lady Melbourne, 'because it was the only chance of redemption for *two* persons. . . .' And, although Augusta had another candidate in mind, it was at this moment that Annabella, as if on cue, told Byron that the (did he but know it, mythical) other candidate for her heart was now no more than a friend. What did he really feel about her?

'I did – do – and always shall love you,' Byron wrote. But at the same time, though he could not help his love, he asked for nothing from her: 'You would probably like me if you could,' he somewhat wanly conceded. Annabella offered him her friendship; Byron suggested that perhaps they ought not to continue writing to each other. She replied that she would end their correspondence only

Joe Murray, the head of
Byron's domestic retainers.

if he found it disagreeable. She went on to ask him about his
projects, his activities, his suggestions for books she might be
reading – it is rarely that any man can resist the temptation either
to talk about himself or to give advice to others. Byron – now with
Augusta at Newstead – sent Annabella a reading list, but told her
it was unlikely he would be able to make his visit to Seaham
before the end of the year. She expressed her disappointment,
her parents' disappointment, and begged him at least to continue
the correspondence. He replied with apparent irritation; yet the
letters continued flitting busily to and fro. Though strained, the
bond between them, whatever it consisted of, did not break.

In the meantime, Byron's financial situation had slightly, and
momentarily, eased. Claughton, the one-time prospective buyer
of Newstead, who had long struggled against paying over any
money as forfeit after his decision to withdraw from the purchase,
was finally persuaded to part with £25,000; and for the first time
Byron, in accepting £700 from John Murray for his poem *Lara*,

had wavered in his high-principled conviction that a gentleman should not take money for his writings. At the same time, Augusta's scheme to get him married failed – her candidate became the wife of the Duke of Norfolk's only son. Yet the need for him to become matrimonially settled pressed as urgently as before.

It was nevertheless somewhat unexpectedly, after a series of rather snappy, irritated letters, that Byron suddenly wrote to Annabella,

A few weeks ago you asked me a question which I answered. I have now one to propose. . . . Are the objections to which you alluded insuperable? or is there any line or change of conduct which could possibly remove them? . . . . I neither wish you to promise or pledge yourself to anything; but merely to learn a *possibility* which would not leave you the less a free agent. . . . With the rest of my sentiments you are already acquainted. If I do not repeat them it is to avoid – or at least not increase – your displeasure.

Was this a proposal? Not one that, Byron must have thought, really committed him to a course of action. Certainly it was less than fiercely ardent, rather cooler than one might have expected from the great lover, the poet, beautiful, romantic, who had raised a thousand illicit hungers in the powdered bosoms of London society. Waiting for Annabella's reply, he even toyed with the idea of a journey to Italy, where Lady Oxford still travelled.

Annabella, not given to many doubts about her value, both absolute in itself and relative to others, did not see Byron's letter as at all tentative. 'I am and have long been pledged to myself to make your happiness my first object in life. . . .' Receiving this, Byron went pale, whether from terror or affection it is hard to say. In any case, on the day of its receipt, 'Your letter has given me a new existence,' he wrote to her '. . . I have ever regarded you as one of the first of human beings. . . . I know your worth – and revere your virtues as I love yourself. . . . It *is* in your power to render me happy – you have made me so already. . . .' The punctuation is wild, the sense veers from a panegyric on her virtues to an attempt at something more passionate, more personal – but it is an attempt that fails. The same day, Byron wrote to Lady Melbourne – 'Miss Milbanke has accepted me. . . . May I hope for your consent, too?' – and to Tom Moore. One gets the feeling from this last letter that he is whistling for a wind, hoping even for a gale to whirl him off to safer waters: 'I am going to be

98

married – that is, I am accepted, and one usually hopes the rest will follow. . . . Miss Milbanke is the lady . . . and you will not deny her judgement, after having refused six suitors and taken on me. . . . Things may occur to break it off, but I will hope not. . . . If this had not happened, I should have gone to Italy. . . .' Does one not detect a slightly forlorn note? 'If this had not happened' – it suggests some accident or sudden illness, rather than a pending marriage.

Yet a marriage it was to be. On 1 November he arrived at Seaham, to be met by the hen-pecked Sir Ralph, the detestable (to Byron) Lady Judith, and by Annabella's brother. Two days later, Byron was writing to Lady Melbourne that 'the die is cast; neither party can recede; the lawyers are here' – nothing now could prevent his becoming 'Lord Annabella'. Yet, as later letters show, he had found some compensation, for Annabella, whatever her puritan convictions, showed herself more amenable to his caresses than he might have expected. He referred to these intimacies as his 'calming process' – and she sometimes needed calming, for she talked a great deal, was often didactic and sometimes censorious, and even at her best seems to have conversed with a high, but dreary, seriousness. They quarrelled at times; once, she reported later, he told her, 'I will be even with you yet!', and this in abrupt reply to her endearments. Did she too, when these episodes occurred, have doubts? She did not express them; on the contrary, she urged swift marriage, rather than a long waiting for the lawyers to draw up the necessary settlement. Byron agreed; he had left Seaham in mid-November. Now, with Hobhouse, he travelled back again. On 2 January 1815, he and Annabella were married. The next day he wrote to Lady Melbourne, addressing her as 'My Dearest Aunt' – 'We were married yesterday at ten upon ye clock, so there's an end of that matter, and the beginning of many others.'

The Separation, a Sketch from the private life of Lord IR

4 Infamy

For Inez call'd some druggists and physicians,
    And tried to prove her loving lord was *mad*,
But as he had some lucid intermissions,
    She next decided he was only *bad* . . .

Ap. 1816.

who Panegyrized his Wife, but Satirized her Confidante !!

ON 15 JANUARY 1816, LADY BYRON took up her baby and left her husband, their house and London; she travelled back to her parents' home and Byron never saw her again. Ever since, the enigma of why she did so, what she really intended, what actually happened between them, has exercised biographers and literary historians. Yet a question in some ways more puzzling is why Byron ever married her. For Annabella seems to have been a humourless and hypocritical prude, an incipient shrew, as her behaviour to her parents showed, a would-be intellectual, sanctimonious, self-justifying, prim, prejudiced and totally encased in a complacent, self-regarding 'virtue'. She was in almost every particular precisely the kind of woman, the kind of person, Byron had always detested. She had neither true beauty nor high spirits to tip the balance in her favour, nor was she in the slightest degree boyish, in a way which might have stimulated Byron's less orthodox fancies. Did she represent a challenge – did he imagine that, just as she thought she could 'reform' him, he could change, subdue, humanise or perhaps even debauch her? 'She is said to be an heiress,' he had written to Tom Moore, but had added, 'of that, I really know nothing certainly, and shall not enquire'. It was not money, then, which drew him. What did? As the coils of her singularly unattractive character unfold in the ensuing years, we can only marvel at the strange folly of genius.

Not that Byron expected much; before the wedding, Hobhouse, the best man, noted in his diary: 'The bridegroom is more and more *less* impatient.' Byron had imagined himself into a marriage; he needed a wife, he had felt, and he had seen himself as a husband, amiable, ordered, happy – automatically reformed. But flesh and blood, and even words and promises, are harder to manage than to imagine. This fantasy bridegroom had to make a real marriage, after all, a matter of rings – his mother's, too large in the event for Annabella – and ceremonies. Not that there were many of the latter: the gathering small – Hobhouse, Annabella's erstwhile governess, Mrs Clermont, a pair of clergymen, the parents; the bride's voice firm, the bridegroom stumbling over the first of his words, then smiling at the irony of 'all my worldly goods'; she reappearing, dressed to travel, and then the couple off, without reception, speeches or prolonged farewells, the coach already rattling across the snow-bound landscape of Yorkshire, on the way to Halnaby Hall and what Byron was to call their 'treacle moon'. Hobhouse recorded: 'I felt as if I had buried a friend.'

If the reasons why Byron chose so unsuitable a wife are

mysterious, even more mysterious are the events marking their one-year marriage. So involved was everyone around him – wife, sister, cousin and all – in the intrigues which followed Lady Byron's final departure, all one can say with certainty is that the marriage began, and that it ended. Did he really sing wildly as they drove along on that first afternoon? Did he really turn to her in fury and tell her she should have married him when he first proposed and that now he would make her suffer for the rejection? Did he really reveal to her then how much he hated her mother? Moore tells us that Byron, according to his Memoirs, had '*had* Lady B. on the sofa before dinner on the day of their marriage' – would she have consented, after such ferocity, such unprovoked anger? If he raped her, she never accused him of it – an unlikely omission, given her later, self-righteously comprehensive indictments. And, as Byron said much later, if he 'had made so uncavalier, not to say brutal a speech, I am convinced Lady Byron would instantly have left the carriage'. If it was mutual passion, however, that brought them so hastily to that pre-prandial couch, can he really have said the things she later accused him of saying? And if he did not, what are we to believe of the rest of Lady Byron's version of her marriage?

It is clear, however, that Byron was moody, unpredictable, given to periods of depression and of undisciplined vivacity, that he was self-indulgent and sensual, that he cared more for the immediate response of wit or anger than the plodding moralising which his wife mistook for penetrating thought. He was often careless of the effect he had on others, bent as he was on finding an outlet for his own feelings. He was touchy, proud, cantankerous, snobbish and vain, he drank too much and ate too irregularly, he had friends of whom almost anyone he could have married might have disapproved. She on the other hand was always serious, convinced that everything he said meant something and that it was her duty to ferret out that meaning. For a man given to striking attitudes, to swift phrases spoken almost before thought, to the malice and cool cynicism of the fashionable, such close attention must have seemed bizarre. Much of what he said was not meant to be considered, only responded to and forgotten. But Annabella could neither respond nor forget.

The day after the marriage he rose late: 'It's too late now – it's done – you should have thought of it sooner,' he said, with cryptic menace, to his wife; later, hinting at the monstrosity of his crimes, he told her, 'I am a villain – I could convince you of it

104

in three words.' He began to compare her, unfavourably, with his sister and when Augusta wrote to him, beginning her letter, 'Dearest, first & best of human beings', he mockingly asked his wife what she thought such endearments might mean. His moods drove him to pace the long gallery of Halnaby Hall night after night, to turn from her at times with a ferocious 'I don't want you', to threaten suicide. And yet, he devised a pet name for her, 'Pippin', and she called him 'Dear Duck'. He wrote to Lady Melbourne, 'Bell and I go on extremely well so far. . . . I have found nothing as yet that I could wish changed for the better.' Was he keeping up appearances – or is her version of what happened so distorted as to be untrue?

After three weeks, the couple travelled to Seaham and there, faced by her father's pointless droning and the ill-informed prattle of her mother, they drew closer together for a while. Early in February, Byron wrote to Tom Moore, 'I still think one ought to marry upon *lease*; but am very sure I should renew mine at the expiration, though next term were for ninety and nine years.' Yet, the moment that, a month later, they were once more alone together in their carriage, Byron's ferocity apparently reappeared. Perhaps this time he had a reason – although he had tried to make the visit on his own, it was both of them who were now on their way to see Augusta; his bitterness may have been increased by the absence of Augusta's husband, Colonel Leigh, and the consequent sense of an opportunity lost.

His behaviour now seems more easily credible, if he is taken to be in love with Augusta. For he sent Annabella to bed early, with the taunt that he and Augusta knew very well how to amuse themselves; in the bedroom, frenzied perhaps by his enforced absence from Augusta's bed, he ranted at his wife; he even hinted, on the first night, that he had just made love to his sister. (She greeted them calmly enough next morning to make this unlikely.) Yet Annabella wrote no word of complaint to her parents and seems to have invited Byron's sister to London within a few days of her own arrival there. Would she really have done so if her own sufferings under Augusta's roof had been so extreme? Perhaps, though, she was trying to humour her husband, who apparently told her she was a fool to issue such an invitation – 'you'll find it will make a great difference to *you* in all ways', a warning which may, after all, have been meant kindly. Settled in Lady Devonshire's house, at 13 Piccadilly Terrace (Byron's normal superstition had been allayed, perhaps, by its having been picked for

him by Lady Melbourne), he sailed out once more into the currents, eddies and whirlpools of London society.

The establishment – servants, carriage, coachman, liveries, accoutrements – which he felt he needed to keep up, as well as his own excesses, brought the problem of money once more pressingly close. Yet he refused to take a penny for his *Hebrew Melodies* – lyrics and love songs rooted in the Bible, but with their heads in Romanticism – though to the publishers they soon brought over £5000. Creditors, made – perhaps properly – ravenous by his fashionable display, descended on him, a motley and vociferous army insisting on their due. But, like others of his station, Byron always thought what was due to them rather less important than what was due to himself, an attitude which did not make their attentions any less worrying. It must have been a relief to be appointed to the Sub-Committee of Management of Drury Lane Theatre and sink himself enjoyably in the toils of its mundane demands – 'C. Bradshaw wants to light the theatre with *gas*. . . . Essex has endeavoured to persuade Kean not to get drunk' – while Lady Byron, at home, balefully considered the possibility that he might instead be in the toils of its younger actresses.

She was now pregnant and keeping much to her room, which he entered, she said later, only briefly and in order to abuse her. Yet that summer Byron's old friend from Harrow, William Harness, had been struck by the harmony between her and her husband and by the attention Byron paid her; Murray was deeply impressed with her; an American visitor thought Byron very affectionate to his wife. When Byron visited Colonel Leigh and Augusta at the end of August, Annabella wrote to him affectionately, hoping he still remembered his 'Dear Pip'. Hobhouse later recalled that it had seemed impossible 'for any couple to live in more apparent harmony; indeed, it was the fear of some friends that his Lordship confined himself too much with Lady Byron'.

The contradictions multiply, but perhaps in a way which offers us a picture complex enough to be true to life: a difficult man, a difficult woman; two egocentrics, though of different temperaments, locked together, one hardly understanding that he made the other suffer, the other unaware that the causes of her suffering lay in his own; a life bewildering to her in its sudden darks and lights, but too even for him, its small happinesses made shoddy by use (Annabella pointed out to Augusta that Byron's 'misfortune is an habitual *passion for Excitement*'), yet a life containing those lights, those happinesses, whatever either of them were later

OPPOSITE Augusta Leigh.
*When fortune changed, and
love fled far,
And hatred's shafts flew
quick and fast,
Thou wert the solitary star
Which rose and set not
to the last.*

Edmund Kean, playing Richard III before George IV at Drury Lane. 'By Jove,' wrote Byron after seeing the performance, 'he is a soul! Life – nature – truth without exaggeration or diminution.'

to assert. Perhaps Fletcher, Byron's old servant, put his finger on the trouble when he said, 'It is very odd, but I never knew a lady that could not manage my Lord, *except* my Lady', though the problem may not have lain only within Annabella's temperament, but also in the fact that she was his wife and thus a limitation upon him, a constraint by nothing more than her mere existence.

The last financial ignominy occurred in November: a bailiff invaded Piccadilly Terrace and settled in the house. In these circumstances of strain, Annabella's pregnancy wore on, with Byron alternating paroxysms of fury with threats to go abroad the moment the child was born. John Murray, apparently unaware of the real state of tension in the household (perhaps a cautionary indication of the value to be placed on outsiders' evidence), had written to Walter Scott that Byron was 'in better dancing spirits than I ever knew him'; now he heard that in his straits Byron was about to sell his library; he sent him a cheque for £1500, but Byron returned it, 'not accepted, but certainly not *unhonoured*'. It was perhaps to escape from the grimness of his marital reality that Byron turned in November to the relative fantasy of adultery. His only known marital infidelity occurred then, his partner a Drury Lane actress named Susan Boyce. She was a girl with pretensions – she thought their involvement a

'natural consequence of two extraordinary beings meeting'. For Byron, however, as he wrote some six years later, she was little more than 'a transient piece of mine'.

Quite apart from this meaningless infidelity, Byron seemed to become wilder in his behaviour as the weeks went by. Even Augusta, who had always been able to manage him better than anyone, who had laughed with and at him until his angers or depressions subsided, now felt it necessary to ask Mrs Clermont, Annabella's one-time governess, and Byron's cousin George to live at Piccadilly Terrace. Thus she, who had herself hurried to town in response to Annabella's alarm over Byron's erratic moods, was forced to call in allies. It seems likely that Byron now did abuse his wife, insulting and threatening her. Indeed, her testimony insists that only three hours before she went into labour, he was saying that he hoped she and the child would die and that if it did not, he would curse it. On the other hand, she also said that during labour he threw bottles at the ceiling of the room below which she was lying; Hobhouse examined that ceiling later and found that it 'retained no marks of blows'.

Kean as Othello.

109

Kirkby Mallory Hall in
Leicestershire.

Early in the afternoon of 10 December Lady Byron gave birth
to a daughter, Augusta Ada. 'Oh, what an implement of torture
have I acquired in you!' was one version of Byron's welcome to
the newborn babe, but according to Augusta, writing the next
day to Francis Hodgson, 'B. is in great good looks, and much
pleased with his *Daughter*, though I believe he would have preferred a *Son*.' Even Mrs Clermont, later so firmly in her one-time
charge's camp, told Hobhouse, according to his own notes, 'that
she had never seen a man so proud and fond of his child as Lord

110

Byron'; he was, as Lady Byron often told him, fonder of it than she was, 'adding also what, to be sure, might have been as well omitted, and "fonder of it than you are of me".'

Worry, and drink to drown worry; intermittent fury at home. To Hobhouse, Byron admitted only one real altercation with his wife: standing before the fire as he came up, 'Am I in your way?' she asked. 'I answered, "Yes, you *are*", with emphasis.' She fled, weeping, he followed 'and begged her pardon *most* humbly'. But he also told Hobhouse that his 'pecuniary embarrassments were such as to drive him *half-mad*', and he was not the man to spare those about him the vehement expression of his frustration and outrage. On 5 January he wrote to Tom Moore, 'I have now been married a year on the second of this month – heigh-ho!' One cannot take this as an expression of domestic contentment.

A day later, he wrote Annabella a note which continued a theme he had begun some time earlier, namely that their Piccadilly house was too expensive to keep and that they should for a while retreat to the country. He wanted them to go first to Kirkby Mallory, where her parents now had their home. 'As the dismissal of the present establishment is of importance to me – the sooner you can fix on a day the better – though of course your convenience & inclination shall be first consulted. . . .' A cold tone, a hard demand; she and Ada were to leave first, while he tidied his affairs as best he could. After a short quarrel, Annabella agreed to go and, according to Byron, 'she herself fixed the day of her departure'. If she did, it makes nonsense of her later claims to have been turned out.

On the other hand, the shortness of the quarrel and her quiet acquiescence in his plans may have been caused by a new conviction which had now seized her – that Byron was insane. She had read in the *Medical Journal* a description of hydrocephalus – 'water on the brain' – and decided she had tracked down the cause of all her, and his, distress. Although the gathering bailiffs might have been a more useful clue, she seems as a result to have felt justified in a number of unmatrimonial actions, of which probably the least appealing was her searching of his private effects. She found a bottle of laudanum and a copy of de Sade's *Justine* and was thus apparently confirmed in her suspicions. No wonder that Byron, who knew nothing of this, was often irritated during her last days at Piccadilly Terrace by her watching him 'with a mixture of pity and anxiety'.

According to Annabella's later recollections, she did not depart without some sentimental moments; she speaks of 'a violent agony of Tears' and of her temptation as she left the house to throw herself on 'a large mat on which his Newfoundland dog used to lie . . . and wait at all hazards'. It is unlikely that Byron could have restrained either his irritation or his sense of humour had she done so and it is as well, perhaps, that this feeling lasted 'only a moment – and I passed on'.

Did Annabella intend at that point to leave her husband? What is one to make of the notes she wrote him, the first while still on the journey?

Dearest B

The child is quite well and the best of travellers. I hope you are *good* and remember my medical prayers and injunctions. Don't give yourself up to the abominable trade of versifying – nor to brandy – nor to anything or anybody that is not *lawful* and *right*.

Though *I* disobey in writing to you, let me hear of *your* obedience at Kirkby.

Ada's love to you with mine.

Pip

Is there a valedictory note there, a sense of final farewells? Certainly there is no hope expressed for an early meeting. And is there an edge in that phrase 'abominable trade of versifying'? 'Trade', to a man as self-consciously an aristocrat as Byron, and one moreover who despite the utmost temptation had refused on almost every occasion to take money for what he had written? But Byron himself spoke disparagingly of literature as a career – at least, when not with literary men. And what of her second letter, addressed to 'Dearest Duck'? Both her father '& Mam long to have the family party completed. . . . If I were not always looking about for B, I should be a great deal better already for the country air. *Miss* finds her provisions increased, & fattens thereon.' The letter ends, 'Ever thy most loving Pippin . . . Pip––ip.'

Yet Mrs Clermont asserted always that when Lady Byron left London she intended never to return to her husband because 'if ever I should be fool enough to be persuaded to return I shall never leave his house alive' and in a letter to a childhood friend she herself said that her note to Byron was a sham: 'I was desired to write from hence – . . . a few lines in the usual form without any notice of serious subjects. . . .' She felt, nevertheless, that if Byron were really insane she had better at least appear to stand by

112

him – 'But were I now to take the final step, whilst the relations are possessed with this idea, they would desert me' – and if, as Augusta had suggested, Byron committed suicide, 'what should I feel?' Yet it was with her that the idea of his madness had begun and she had left behind in Byron's house a most enthusiastic and efficient spy, one Byron would never – did never – suspect: Augusta Leigh.

Was Augusta, vulnerable to charges of incest, blackmailed into such assistance by Annabella? Or did she imagine that, if Byron could be proved insane, no hint of that scandal would ever emerge? Whatever the reason, she threw herself into the work of espionage, sometimes writing to Annabella, her 'Dear Sis', several times a day, each time offering some suitable titbit of information – Byron had had a pistol out, because he had seen someone lurking suspiciously in the street; Byron had come home drunk with Hobhouse and they had talked extremely loudly; Byron had asked Dr Le Mann whether a bad liver could make one a hypochondriac.

And Byron himself? He seems to have been broody and de-spondent, when not either carousing or recovering from carous-ing, worried about his health and about money – yet he admitted that Annabella was the only woman he could have lived with for even six months and he read her letters over and over again. She, meanwhile, was writing to George Byron that she and her parents thought 'the Patient', as she now called Byron, ought to join her in Kirkby Mallory, for her parents wished to give him all possible care and attention. As always, the picture is confused.

It becomes clearer, however, almost at once, for within days Lady Judith, Annabella's mother, had come to London to present to lawyers a statement her daughter had made; the long hounding of Byron had begun. If there was a change of mind, one must won-der what induced it. What suddenly made Annabella and her parents so virtuously vicious, what changed her from hoping on 17 January that 'the Patient' would come and benefit from country air and exercise, to drawing up two days later what amounted to an indictment against her husband, and a day after that setting out her reasons for making their separation permanent? (Her logic is precise: if he was mentally sick, she was his chief victim and so least qualified to stay with him; if he was wicked, she need not hesitate to leave him; if he was simply weak and ill-counselled, why should she remain when the future would doubtless only repeat the miseries of the past? 'Princess of Parellellograms'

The drawing-room at 50
Albemarle Street, premises
of Byron's publisher, John
Murray. Byron is seen
talking to Sir Walter Scott
in the window alcove.

indeed!) By the time Byron's birthday, on 22 January, came, Annabella was warning her mother, now in London, that her husband must have no notion of the plots against him, for otherwise he might neither confirm that her own behaviour had been above suspicion nor make provision for the child. (At the same time she had taken the logic of self-justification further, suggesting that it was remorse at having used her so shamefully which was driving Byron to madness; it was therefore actually in his interest if he never saw her again.) What had caused this alteration of mood, this formation of so united and granite an anti-Byron front?

It is hard not to assume a conversation, perhaps on 18 January, a council of war and a new resolve arising from it, possibly because of some revelation by Annabella. What might this have been? Byron's incest with Augusta? That might have produced Lady Judith's revulsion, but Annabella had been living with the knowledge for months. There has been another suggestion, most notably by G. Wilson Knight in his *Lord Byron's Marriage* (but rejected since by Doris Langley Moore) – that we should take seriously *Don Leon*, an obscene but persuasive poem written by George Coleman the Younger, a friend and drinking-companion of the never-reticent Byron. The reason he gives for the separation is an act of anal intercourse carried out by Byron on his wife during the last month of her pregnancy. It seems likely that for a young woman like Annabella, learned yet unsophisticated, such a sexual approach would have been something literally unheard of. In her ignorance, she might well not have known what to think of it – until told by someone else what the proper reaction should have been. Indeed, one can quite easily imagine her offering the information almost innocently, as just another piece of evidence confirming Byron's disturbed state of mind. Certainly Byron agreed years later that his wife's friends had accused him of the crime of Jacopo Rusticucci, whom Dante set in his *Inferno* among those tormented for the crime of sodomy.

By 24 January Annabella, still without telling Byron, was authorising her mother to take whatever steps were necessary to ensure the separation; madness, however, though possibly Byron's malady, could not be proved sufficiently to make it the grounds. Better to make his hatred of her the basis of her plea. Four days later, a letter from Sir Ralph arrived at Piccadilly Terrace – a letter examined, redrafted and refined by lawyers, at last informing Byron of what was being decided. But Augusta unaccountably returned it unopened, earning the undying

116

detestation of Lady Judith for doing so. Thus, still in ignorance of the complicated plotting which involved most of those in contact with his household, Byron ordered horses to take him to Kirkby the following week-end. It was only at this point, on 2 February, that he received the letter from Sir Ralph.

Byron, astonished and bewildered, refused to believe that its demand for a separation was actually Annabella's wish, but saw it as some parental machination of which she too was the victim. He ought perhaps to have remembered how low in the pecking-order Sir Ralph actually stood. He replied, pointing out that, from his point of view, there was nothing in Annabella's behaviour which could be improved and asking her to write and tell him what she herself wanted. Intent as always on ferreting out hidden meanings, she sent his letter to her lawyer, Lushington. Byron wrote again, more urgently: 'Dearest Bell . . . do recollect – that all is at stake – the present – the future – & even the colouring of the past.' He insisted that he loved her '& will not part from you without your *own* most express and *expressed* refusal to return or receive me . . . ever yours dearest most'.

Did Byron deceive himself, imagining for present use feelings from a fantasised past? It was not his custom to be dishonest, yet he was a man swept along by his most immediate responses. In any case, he warmed no cockle in Annabella's virtuous heart. She replied to him with a lofty self-righteousness: only her own convictions had dictated her conduct; she had been loyal although persecuted; finally her misery had brought her to the decision to part from him. 'Were you, then, *never* happy with me?' he asked her desperately.

By now, Caroline Lamb, perhaps seeing at last a chance for revenge, was dropping dark hints of what Hobhouse records only as Byron's '————', which might refer to his homosexuality, or possibly to the sodomy of which Coleman was to write. Annabella remained, as was her nature, adamant. In answer to Byron's repeated pleas, made both to her and to others, she wrote, 'It can be fully and clearly proved that I left your house under the persuasion of your having a complaint of so dangerous a nature that any agitation might bring on a fatal crisis.' Her absence had been 'medically recommended', but she had intended to have him join her at Kirkby, where 'I would have devoted myself to the alleviation of *your* sufferings, and should not then have reminded you of *my own*. . . .' However, he was not mad: 'I cannot attribute your "state of mind" to any cause so much as the *total* dereliction

117

Illustrations from *The Dream*. OPPOSITE
There was an ancient mansion, and before
Its wall there was a steed, caparison'd . . .

ABOVE *. . . and in the last he lay*
Reposing from the noontide sultriness
Couch'd among fallen columns . . .

of principle. . . . I have *consistently* fulfilled my duty as your wife. It was too dear to be resigned till it became hopeless. Now my resolution cannot be changed.'

'I know not what to say,' Byron told her in mid-February, 'every step appears to bear you further from me. . . . I can only say in the truth of affliction, and without hope, motive or end in again saying what I have lately but vainly repeated, that I love you, bad or good, mad or rational, miserable or content, I love you, and shall do, to the dregs of my memory and existence.' But Annabella was busily pursuing her own course, preparing to come to London – a London where the separation and its probable causes was now the major source of fashionable conversation – in order to offer her lawyer, Lushington, details she alone, she insisted, could give him personally. And when she came at the end of the month, what did she tell him? About the incest, most people have assumed, and it is probable; but she may well have thought Byron's 'unnatural' act something which could be used as a weapon against him. Certainly it is reported that those who later saw parts of her second statement found them coarse and even nauseating, a reaction not even the sensitive Henry James, one of these later readers, would have had in the face of simple incest.

By now, though, stories of the incest had entered the mainstream of gossip, to the horror of Hobhouse, to whom they were evidently new. It was, perhaps, Lady Caroline Lamb who had begun to spread them; one can imagine her dancing with glee on the shreds of Byron's reputation. She was writing to both Byron and his wife, promising support for him – and for her, revelations. Byron, despondent and almost ruined, bailiffs in charge of his library, was in no mood for another bout of Caroline's excesses. To Tom Moore he wrote, 'I do not know that . . . I was ever, at home or abroad, in a situation so completely uprooting of present pleasure, or rational hope for the future. . . .' Now the struggle began over the separation agreement; despite Lord Holland's acting as intermediary, Byron's first reaction was to insist that only one agreement was possible – that of his wife to return to him. She, however, reminded him that he had once promised his consent 'to a private Agreement' if he was convinced the separation had been of her free will. That Augusta was now near breakdown must have contributed to Annabella's comfort – her year of jealousy was being pleasantly revenged. By the end of March, Augusta had left Byron's house and Byron had agreed to the terms of the separation. In a mood of unexpected and abrupt

OPPOSITE *The Bride of Abydos*, by Eugène Delacroix.

euphoria, he prepared to travel abroad.

Annabella pursued her relentless course. Caroline Lamb met her and told her, among other things, of Byron's 'practice of unnatural crime' – Rushton was named and '3 schoolfellows whom he had thus perverted'. She reported this to Lushington, who replied by congratulating her 'upon your final escape from all proximity to or intercourse with such contamination'. Byron's library was sold, his friends – Hobhouse, Murray and others –

A Regency dinner in John Nash's banqueting room in the
Brighton Pavilion.

buying what they could; Byron himself was undergoing the new experience of being publicly shunned in the salons and drawing-rooms which he had once so dramatically mastered.

Yet there was now a new direction in Byron's life; Europe beckoned . . . and a new mistress who, though in herself to be of no great importance in his life, would lead him on to other and more significant associations. He had, at the height of his distress, received a letter from her – 'An utter stranger takes the liberty of addressing you. . . . There are cases where virtue may stoop to assume the garb of folly; it is for the piercing eye of genius to penetrate the disguise. . . .' It was signed 'E. Trefusis'; Byron did not answer it. Another note came, only initialled this time: 'Lord Byron is requested to state whether seven o'clock this Evening will be convenient to him to receive a lady to communicate with him on business of peculiar importance. She desires to be admitted alone. . . .' It was in this way that he met – and did not fall in love with – Mary Jane Clairmont, who had by now adopted the Christian name 'Claire'. What was to be important in Byron's life was that she was step-sister to Mary Godwin, soon to be Shelley's wife. Claire continued to pursue him and although she was twice turned away from his house, she eventually became his mistress. By mid-April, she was pregnant.

Byron, unaware of this, was already actively preparing to leave a London where, so Annabella wrote to her mother, the good were being distinguished from the wicked by whether they shunned Byron or not. Perhaps still unaware of the malice she bore him and which her glee at this expressed, he wrote to her again. He had just parted, he said, from Augusta, 'almost the last being you have left me to part with'. (He was, of course, still ignorant of his half-sister's role as double-agent.) 'Wherever I may go, – and I am going far, – you and I can never meet in this world, nor the next.' He asked her, however, to be kind to Augusta, 'for never has she acted or spoken towards you but as your friend'. The rest is cool, the content the minutiae of their arrangements – 'The carriage is yours. . . . The receipts can remain. . . . My address will be left with Mrs Leigh. . . . The ring . . . I wish to be preserved to Miss Byron. . . . Yours truly, Byron.'

Then he was away, on 23 April – and away early, for the Duchess of Devonshire was sending in the bailiffs to sequestrate whatever of his belongings was left to take and hold. Byron had with him as companion Dr Polidori, a young physician twenty-one years old; he felt he needed a constant medical attendant.

125

RIGHT Dr John William Polidori, whom Byron engaged as his personal physician before leaving England. He dismissed him, however, after a few months for 'he had an alacrity of getting into scrapes, and was too young and heedless'.

OPPOSITE Byron on leaving England.
I go – but wheresoe'er I flee,
There's not an eye will
weep for me . . .

Polidori was a man of great vanity, short on sensitivity and with his own literary ambitions and later Byron was to feel he had made a mistake in travelling with him. Now, however, it was all bustle as, with Rushton and Fletcher as ever in attendance, and a Swiss servant named Berger, they took the road to Dover. That seaside town was instantly agog; it was reported that its ladies dressed as chambermaids in order to get a good, close look at the notorious poet. For a day there was a contrary wind; then a change, a good tide, Byron aboard, Hobhouse and Scrope Davies to see him off, hurrying to the end of the pier for a last glimpse of him on the afterdeck, where, Hobhouse records, 'the dear fellow pulled off his cap & wav'd it to me – I gazed until I could not distinguish him any longer – God bless him for a gallant spirit and a kind one. . . .'

126

Lord Byron

5 Exile

The waters heave around me; and on high
The winds lift up their voices: I depart,
Whither I know not; but the hour's gone by,
When Albion's lessening shores could grieve or glad mine eye.

ENICE HIS PROBABLE DESTINATION, Byron was nevertheless in no hurry; abroad, he felt once more a liberated being. ('As soon as he reached his room, Lord Byron fell like a thunderbolt upon the chambermaid,' Dr Polidori recorded in Belgium, perhaps by way of medical observation.) Ostend, Brussels, Waterloo, that battlefield only one year into history, still spattered with the shards of a gigantic reputation; then on down the Rhine, the crags and castles of Childe Harold's origins at last visited in the flesh. Finally, Byron in his vast travelling coach – modelled on Napoleon's – descended on Geneva, where Claire Clairmont awaited him with some impatience. With her were Shelley and Mary Godwin.

Although Byron took up only with the utmost reluctance – and under her unremitting and immodest pressure – his old relationship with Claire, he settled with instant delight into friendship with Shelley. Soon, renting the Villa Diodati, he had become Shelley's neighbour and there now began an almost continuous conversation, talk taken up nightly and long into the night, discussion, speculation, statement, argument, humour, philosophy, criticism, Shelley opening for Byron an ethereal vision different from anything he had imagined hitherto (he was even for a while reconciled to the works of Wordsworth, which he loathed). The moment and the vision passed – Byron was a man who found the ether heavy going, moving swiftest on the earth. Shelley nevertheless became convinced from this time on that Byron was the most extraordinary man, the most extraordinary poet, of the age.

But despite all the talk and laughter, despite all the sailing he and Shelley did on the great lake by which their houses stood, despite the tours they made, Byron continued as always to work. 'Tell Murray I have a 3rd Canto of Childe Harold finished,' he wrote to Hobhouse in June. And, his libertarian spirit moved by the grim battlements of the castle at Chillon, where heretics both religious and secular had once been kept in chains, he wrote The Prisoner of Chillon, soon one of the most popular of his shorter poems.

In London, meanwhile, Annabella became more and more grimly determined to prove Byron's incest (perhaps to avoid admitting that the real cause of the separation was an act in which she would also have taken part). She needed Augusta's confession, but Augusta was different from her brother whose hauntingly Calvinistic upbringing she had avoided, and Annabella noted in a letter to a confidante that 'his feelings – distinct from practice – were much more sensitive & correct on all moral questions than hers. She did not appear to think these transgressions *of conse-*

PREVIOUS PAGES
I stood in Venice, on the
Bridge of Sighs;
A palace and a prison on
each hand:
I saw from out the wave her
structures rise
As from the stroke of the
enchanter's wand . . .

OPPOSITE Claire Clairmont.
'I was not in love,' wrote
Byron to Augusta, 'nor have
I any love left for any, but
I could not exactly play the
Stoic with a woman who had
scrambled eight hundred
miles to unphilosophize
me. . . .'

130

quence.' Literate London, in the meantime, in its continuing discussion of Byron's more bizarre characteristics, received some assistance from the thinly disguised portrait of him drawn by Caroline Lamb in her novel *Glenarvon*. Byron, however, lent the book by Madame de Staël in faraway Geneva, said only, 'As for the likeness, the picture can't be good – I did not sit long enough!'

Tired of keeping at bay the importunate Claire, he must have been delighted to see Shelley's party leave for England on 29 August. Claire wrote him a final letter: 'Farewell my dearest dear Lord Byron,' she began, and assured him, 'dearest I shall love you to the end of my life & nobody else. . . .', a sad note, especially when contrasted with Byron's description of her to his sister – 'a foolish girl . . . I have had all the plague possible to persuade her to go back again; but at last she went. . . . I was not in love . . . but I could not exactly play the Stoic with a woman who had scrambled eight hundred miles to unphilosophize me.'

Byron, too, travelled on, jettisoning Rushton and, less successfully, Polidori on the way, but taking the visiting Hobhouse with him to the Bernese Alps. In a journal he kept for Augusta, he wrote, 'Passed *whole woods of withered pines, all withered*. . . . – their appearance reminded me of me and my family.' He had already written to her, 'I shall never find anyone like you – nor you (vain as it may seem) like me.' Yet by then Augusta's defences had been so eroded by Annabella that she had even yielded up Byron's letters: 'they are *absolute love letters*,' Annabella recorded gleefully. On Lake Geneva, Byron, for whom 'neither the music of the Shepherd, the crashing of the Avalanche, nor the torrent, the mountain, the Glacier, the Forest, nor the Cloud, have for one moment lightened the weight upon my heart', settled down to wrestle with his own despair in the only way he knew: *Manfred*, a long poetic drama in which the hero first conjures up, then challenges, a range of spirits and atavistic forces, wraiths rooted in his own mind, would appear the following year in London. By then, Byron was in Italy.

In October, in Milan, he heard from Augusta that they could never in future be as intimate as they had been in the past; she did not tell him why – that, hounded by Annabella, she had promised as much. Byron was dumbfounded and bewildered. She was, he wrote to her, 'the only comfort (except the remote possibility of my daughter's being so) left me in prospect in existence. . . .' He went on self-pityingly to describe himself: 'My hair is growing grey, & *not* thicker; & my teeth are sometimes *looseish* though still

132

Byron at the Villa Diodati on
the shore of Lake Leman.

134

white & sound. Would not one think I was sixty instead of not quite nine & twenty?'

But in Venice, which he reached in mid-November, Byron's spirits rose; he delighted in that strange water-lapped city from the first. It had, he told Tom Moore, 'always been (next to the East) the greenest island of my imagination. It has not disappointed me. . . . Besides, I have fallen in love. . . .' He had taken apartments above a draper's shop; the draper had a twenty-two-year-old wife, Marianna; her appearance was 'altogether like an antelope', with 'large, black, oriental eyes'; and, as he told Murray 'her great merit is finding out mine – there is nothing so amiable as discernment'. He also began studying Armenian – 'the most difficult thing I could discover here for an amusement' – and felt that he was well set-up for the winter. 'The lady has, luckily for me, been less obdurate than the language. . . .'

In London, his ghost stalked once more, revived this time by the publication of the Third Canto of *Childe Harold*; such a ghost, its talents overwhelming, London was happy to accept. Murray, who had given Byron £2000 for the copyright of this poem and *The Prisoner of Chillon*, sold the booksellers seven thousand copies of each work during a single evening. Byron meanwhile was apparently little disturbed by the birth of a daughter to Claire Clairmont: 'This comes of "putting it about" (as Jackson calls it)', he wrote, 'and be damned to it – and thus people come into the world.'

With the Carnival to provide a kaleidoscopic and amoral background to his dissipations, Venice suited him; nevertheless as time passed a lassitude, a sort of boredom, overcame him. Marianna absorbed him – and yet not quite enough. In April 1817 he was on the move again, visiting Ferrara and Florence and ending in Rome, where Hobhouse eagerly awaited him. Soon the two of them were riding the slopes of those famous hills, intent on the antique and the strange – and on avoiding the censorious English, many of whom in their gentility found the mere presence of Byron an embarrassment. ('Don't look at him, he is dangerous to look at,' Lady Liddell hissed at her daughter as they neared him in St Peter's.) It was a refreshed Byron who, towards the end of May, made his way back to the dark-eyed Marianna.

He had begun to realise that it was unlikely that he would ever return to England. Augusta had become too nervous for their old association to continue and his homeland now held no other lures. He took a small palace for the summer, in a village a few miles

OPPOSITE The castle of Chillon.
Lake Leman lies by Chillon's
walls:
A thousand feet in depth
below
Its massy waters meet and
flow . . .

LEFT Mary Shelley, the author of *Frankenstein*. BELOW Madame de Staël as Corinne, the heroine in one of her novels. Byron, who was a frequent visitor at the Château de Coppet, across the lake from Diodati, said that 'she writes octavos and talks folios'.

OPPOSITE Shelley. His friendship with Byron was to become one of the most famous in history. After Shelley's death, Byron wrote to Thomas Moore: 'You were all brutally mistaken about Shelley, who was, without exception, the best and least selfish man I ever knew. I never knew one who was not a beast in comparison.'

Geneva from Coligny where
the Villa Diodati was
situated.
*Clear, placid Leman! thy
           contrasted lake,
With the wild world I
           dwelt in, is a thing
Which warns me, with its
           stillness, to forsake
Earth's troubled waters
           for a purer spring.*

140

OPPOSITE Venice from San Giorgio Maggiore.
Oh Venice! Venice! when thy marble walls
Are level with the waters, there shall be
A cry of nation o'er thy sunken halls,
A loud lament along the sweeping sea!

RIGHT Byron and Marianna Segati. 'She does not plague me (which is a wonder) and I verily believe we are one of the happiest unlawful couples on this side of the Alps.'

from Venice itself, and there he began working on the last Canto of *Childe Harold*, this now based on his Venetian and Roman experiences, the descriptions marvellous, the mood as darkly, passionately melancholy as before. His life was pleasant now, and regular, his mornings spent in bed, his days on the Lido, his evenings on horseback, his nights working. At the end of July the constant Hobhouse joined him, and it was in his company that he met Margarita Cogni, a baker's wife – 'very dark, tall, the Venetian face, very fine black eyes – and certain other qualities which need not be mentioned.' Challenged by Marianna, she told her rival, '*You* are *not* his *wife*: I am *not* his *wife* . . . *your* husband is a cuckold, and *mine* is another . . . if he prefers what is mine to what is yours, is it my fault?'

At the same time, he made another new beginning. Perhaps he

felt he had failed at becoming the man his poems had described. Now he made his poetry conform to the man he was. Abruptly, the formalised, and to our eyes falsifying, romanticism, the high-flown language, the studied emotions disappear, and in their place we get the raciness and good-humoured cynicism of Byron's letters and conversation. The result was a mock-heroic poem, *Beppo*, the first edition of which, published anonymously in London, proved so successful even the cautious Byron had no objections to putting his name to subsequent printings. Nor did this complete his reasons for contentment. Back in Venice in November, he learned that Newstead had at last been sold, for £94,500. This was enough to clear his debts, now standing at over £30,000, and, with the money he no longer disdained to earn with his writings, to guarantee him a viable and permanent income.

Hobhouse started his journey home early in January 1819, the

OPPOSITE John Cam Hobhouse, later Lord Broughton, Byron's 'guide, philosopher and friend'.

ABOVE A view of Rome, by Samuel Palmer. 'As a whole,' wrote Byron, '*ancient* and *modern*, it beats Greece, Constantinople, everything – at least that I have ever seen.'

last part of *Childe Harold* in his baggage; unchaperoned, therefore, Byron could now set himself for the excesses of the Carnival. As when Hobhouse had left him during their first voyage, Byron seems to have felt an almost savage sense of release. Six weeks later he was writing to Hobhouse that he 'was clapt . . . to be sure it was gratis, the first gonorrhea I have not paid for'. Yet soon the women were coming and going again, mostly from the lower classes, easily persuaded, as easily discarded. Margarita Cogni, however, remained, a sort of sensual *continuo* to the brief solos in the foreground. Marianna had by now been left behind, a decision of the heart which necessitated a change of location, since he could not remain in the apartments above her husband's shop. He rented instead the Palazzo Mocenigo, a vast, rambling building within sight of the Rialto Bridge, damp and, standing as it did beside the Grand Canal, tainted by the insistent miasma which, then as now, rose from the waterways of Venice.

In April Shelley, with his wife, Claire and her daughter, Allegra, and Elise, the baby's Swiss nurse, were in Milan. Byron would not move from Venice, yet was, characteristically, pleased at the prospect of seeing his daughter. Soon, Allegra had joined him and one imagines her, wide-eyed in the clutter of sparsely furnished rooms and corridors, staring from the arms of her nurse into the blue, over-intense eyes of her father, smiling perhaps, reaching out a hand – winning, in any case, his slightly reluctant affection. He told Augusta that she was 'remarkably intelligent, and a great favourite with everybody'; to his astonishment, he found her 'much more like Lady Byron than her mother'; this may have been factually true but is just as likely to have been compensation for his loss of Ada, which by this time he probably felt more deeply than the separation from his wife. Now that he had the space, he also allowed himself another of his characteristic, though less well-known, pleasures – 'I have got two monkeys, a fox, and two mastiffs,' he reported; with such a delight in animals, it is perhaps no wonder that he kept fourteen servants in his establishment, the most notable the ferocious, piratically bearded 'Tita', his gondolier.

Yet nothing prevented his working. Mistresses, English visitors, animals, daughter, not even his gathering indignation, perhaps a little paranoic and a measure of his fretful loneliness, at the paucity of letters from his friends in England, nothing really prevented his diving nightly into the absorbed and lamp-lit calm in which he translated, while others slept, his adventures in their

OPPOSITE Margarita Cogni. 'I am sure if I put a poniard into the hand of this one, she would plunge it where I told her, – and into *me* if I offended her. I like this kind of animal, and am sure that I should have preferred Medea to any woman that ever breathed.'

147

The Palazzo Mocenigo, on the Grand Canal, Byron's residence in Venice.

world into those of his own – that exaggerated, racy, fanciful and witty world he was so busily creating. For now he had begun the vast poem on which his fame mainly rests; with the happy acceptance of *Beppo* as his springboard, he had leaped forward again, into the first lines – 'I want a hero: an uncommon want,/ When every year and month sends forth a new one' – of his great spoof-epic, the vast rumbustious satire *Don Juan*. As always, he used his own experiences – but this time to make his readers laugh. Annabella figured early, as Donna Inez, Juan's mother – 'Oh! she was perfect past all parallel. . . .' – and others who had wandered into his life, to great or small effect, were to appear in its stanzas, sometimes disguised and sometimes named.

Yet still his zest, as always, spilled over into what, as always, he called love. In a letter explaining that he had spent much more money than he might have, he pointed out that, of such expendi-

Allegra: 'she is very pretty,' wrote Byron to Augusta, 'remarkably intelligent, and a great favourite with everybody; but, what is remarkable, much more like Lady Byron than her mother . . . she has very blue eyes and that singular forehead, fair curly hair, and a devil of a Spirit – but that is Papa's.'

ture, 'more than half was laid out on the Sex; – to be sure I have had plenty for the money, that's certain – I think at least two hundred of one sort or another – perhaps more, for I have not lately kept the recount'. To these slightly sordid exploits the world responded with its usual buzzing; Murray in London showed Byron's admittedly over-explicit and perhaps boastful letters to his friends, while all Venice discussed the doings – and excesses – of the notorious British aristocrat. One feels that Byron, always listening for the echoes his existence raised on the blank escarpments of the world, was not displeased to have so widespread a reputation. Yet he must have felt even more alone, even more cut off from England, when he heard of the death of Lady Melbourne early in April.

In August Shelley arrived, with Claire under his wing, drawn to Venice by complaining letters Elise had been sending her; the lurid stories of Byron's Venetian eccentricities with which both gondoliers and waiters immediately regaled the party cannot have eased her mind. It was decided that Claire's presence in Venice should be kept a secret from Byron, a man easily incensed and concerned to keep his distance from her. Yet Byron agreed amenably enough that Claire should see her child: 'If Claire likes to take it, let her take it.' He was less equable later, when he learned Claire was near him; he wrote to Augusta that Allegra's mother '(whom the Devil confound) came prancing the other day over the Appenines. . . .' Yet he found Shelley's company agreeable, perhaps because it had been months since he had been able to speak with anyone truly his equal. Shelley, at first just as delighted, was soon less happy, later describing the women who clustered about Byron as 'perhaps the most contemptible of all who exist under the moon – the most ignorant, the most disgusting, the most bigoted. . . .'

The only durable one of these had at last been turned away – Margarita Cogni, the baker's wife, 'tall and energetic as a Pythoness', who agreed to leave only after extravagant manœuvres with a sharp knife and a desperate dive into the Canal. It was around this period that Hanson arrived, with documents for signature (Byron, asked to meet him, had refused once more to move from Venice) and described what consequences Byron's life was having: 'Lord Byron . . . looked 40. His face had become pale, bloated and sallow. He had grown very fat, his shoulders broad and round, and the knuckles of his hands were lost in fat.' His hair was thinner now, long and curling, but greying, and his one-time modishness had declined into an out-of-date foppishness which was in danger of becoming absurd.

Byron, however, was also a poet; he was eagerly awaiting the response of his friends to the manuscript of the first part of *Don Juan*. Their consensus was not comforting, for, though they praised it, they thought it so free, so coarse in some places and vitriolic in others, that it could not be published. Byron responded vigorously, writing to Murray, 'If they had told me the poetry was bad, I would have acquiesced; but they say the contrary, and then talk to me about morality. . . .' Despite earlier hesitations, he now insisted on publication, and was fortunate in having Murray's enthusiastic support. With some boldness these two decided to fight against the encroaching gloom of a careful, prurient and humourless censoriousness (though Victoria was still a quarter-century away) and bring the poem out.

The *salon* of the Countess Benzoni was one of the stable elements in Byron's life in Venice, a point of constant contact with the relatively respectable elements in Venetian society (though Moore described her as 'thoroughly profligate'). Although now often bored, uncertain whether to stay in Venice or to leave, bemused as to how he should occupy the coming years, conscious of having reached the end of that transient marvel, his youth, Byron continued his visits to the Benzoni evenings, despite giving up much else which had previously amused him.

It was there, early in April 1819, that he first saw the young woman who would preoccupy him for most of the rest of his life: Teresa Guiccioli. Small, but with a full, voluptuous figure, her

Byron in Venice. 'My hair is going grey, and *not* thicker; and my teeth are sometimes looseish though still white & sound. Would not one think I was sixty instead of not quite nine & twenty?'

151

auburn hair fashionably curling to her shoulders, her complexion clear and seemingly radiant, her eyes large and almost indiscreetly soft, she soon attracted his attention, and he hers.

She was nineteen years old and had been married the year before to Count Alessandro Guiccioli, from Ravenna. He was a wily, strong-willed opportunist, manipulating circumstance when this was possible and, when it was not, resorting to force. His first wife had made him rich, and he was suspected of having murdered her. His second had borne him six children while still his servant. When he married her, she died. A year later, he married Teresa. This proved in some ways a mistake, for the known political sympathies of her father and brother threatened to restrict his freedom of manœuvre. Both these men – Count Ruggero Gamba and his son Pietro – were liberal revolutionaries and members of the Carbonari, that mysterious secret society members of which permeated Italy, and were therefore watched by the police with all the intensity of official paranoia.

On that first evening, Byron had not wanted to be introduced to her – he did not want to meet any more women, 'if they are ugly because they are ugly, and if they are beautiful because they are beautiful'. But from their subsequent conversation 'she rose to leave as if in a dream', as she later wrote in that strange third-person narrative, her *Vie de Lord Byron*. And in a confession she seems oddly to have prepared for her husband, she admits, 'I then felt attracted to him by an irresistible force. He became aware of it, and asked to see me alone the next day. I was so imprudent as to agree. . . . I was strong enough to resist at that first encounter, but was so imprudent as to repeat it the next day, when my strength gave way – for B. was not a man to confine himself to sentiment.'

After this they met frequently, but it is less certain that Byron was as instantly bewitched. A few days later he was writing to Hobhouse, 'She is pretty, but has no tact . . . and this blessed night horrified a correct company at the Benzona's [sic] by calling out to me *mio Byron* in an audible key. . . .' In Venice, as elsewhere in polite society, self-indulgence and even genuine passion were circumscribed by accepted conventions. Young girls remained virgin until marriage released them for love. It was then that they looked for an *amico*; the position of the *cavalier servente*, the lover who was always – restrained, obliging – at his lady's side, had become a social institution, a sort of auxiliary husband who behaved according to strict rules. It was a role Byron always detested.

After ten hectic days, the Count took Teresa home to Ravenna;

Teresa Guiccioli

Byron, who seems always to have needed the invisible third person to make him feel that even his most genuine emotions were real, wrote to a friend that they had had 'but ten days to manage all our little matters . . .; and we managed them; and I have done my duty with the proper consummation'. The lovers corresponded with the aid as go-between of an obliging priest named Perelli. Masked now in Italian, Byron could allow himself the full rhetoric of passion:

My dearest Love: Your dearest letter came today . . . it will be difficult for me to reply in your beautiful language to your sweet expressions, which deserve an answer in deeds, rather than words. . . . You, who are my only and last love, who are my only joy, the delight of my life – you who are my only hope – you who were – at least for a moment – all mine – you have gone away. . . . You sometimes tell me that I have been your *first* real love – and I assure you you shall be my last Passion. . . .

There was nevertheless a period of hesitation now, as the letters passed to and fro. Teresa was not entirely clear about what she wanted him to do; he himself seems to have given more than a passing thought to returning to England. On 1 June, however, Byron left for Ravenna, replying to Hobhouse's manifest unease at the dangers of this liaison, 'For anything I know, the affair may terminate in some such way you hint at, for they are liberal with the knife in R.' However, despite Guiccioli's being 'shrewdly suspected of two assassinations already', Byron held to his opinion that 'everything is to be risked for a woman one likes'.

Teresa, who had had a miscarriage, revived remarkably with Byron's arrival. But their meetings were frustrating: 'You are so surrounded,' Byron complained, and 'If you knew what it cost me to control myself in your presence!' As her health improved, this torment was naturally eased, though not without raising new problems, for, as he reported, there was '*no* place but the great Saloon of his own palace – so that if I come away with a Stiletto in my gizzard some fine afternoon – I shall not be astonished. . . .' Yet, for all this half-cynical delight in the danger, something had been renewed in Byron, or perhaps even created for the first time.

'I am in love, and tired of promiscuous concubinage,' he had written to Hobhouse, 'and now have the opportunity of settling for life.' He wrote to another friend, 'If any thing happens to my present *Amica*, I have done with the passion for ever – it is my

OPPOSITE Byron and Teresa Guiccioli. 'I have settled into a regular *serventismo*, and find it the happiest state of all. . . .'

157

last love', and while he was given to self-dramatisation, and to believing permanent his momentary convictions, one may accept, if only from the length, serenity and completeness of the relationship which followed, that he was being as sincere as he knew how. Two years of largely mindless debauchery in which he had misused the words 'love' and 'passion' almost as damagingly as he had his body, had perhaps left him ready for one more, one last attempt at genuine feeling. Perhaps, too, he felt time and its opportunities closing in – he described himself as 'half grey' and added that 'the Crow's-foot has been rather lavish of its indelible steps. My hair, though not gone, seems going, and my teeth remain by way of courtesy. . . .'

In mid-July, two poems were on Byron's mind. The first was *Don Juan* which, misunderstood and in some quarters vilified, seemed to be heading for failure. Murray, disturbed, asked Byron how he planned the poem to continue, and received the even more disturbing reply that Byron had no plan and thought him 'too earnest and eager about a work never intended to be serious. Do you suppose that I could have any intention but to giggle and make giggle?' In the other poem, however, Byron was himself the butt, for in the streets of Ravenna obscene verses were now being sung about him, Teresa and the cuckolded Count.

Abruptly, Guiccioli announced that he was taking Teresa to Bologna, where he had business. On 10 August Byron arrived there, too, having followed them despite a slight unease as to the real intentions of this once-murderous husband. Yet, in fact, Count Guiccioli was tolerant enough, either because the tradition of *cavalier servente* was so well established that he could see no alternative, or because he felt that Byron might at some time prove useful; certainly he asked him for help in obtaining the post of British consul, valuable in giving status during periods of political upheaval.

Byron, still struggling with his feelings, wrote to Hobhouse, 'I feel – and feel it bitterly – that a man should not consume his life at the side and on the bosom of a woman, and a stranger. . . . But I have neither the strength of mind to break my chain, nor the insensibility which would deaden its weight.' He wrote this during a short separation from Teresa; as soon as she returned, with that immediacy of response which always charmed others and so often nearly destroyed him, his tranquillity returned.

As though to give his household a greater stability, Allegra had also arrived. He wrote to Augusta that she 'has a good deal of the

Byron' and it is clear from the tone of his letters that he was delighted with her. His situation had also been, somewhat astonishingly, regularised by the Count's offering him an apartment in his *palazzo* – although Byron, hesitating before accepting, may have felt there was an element of risk in the move. Count Guiccioli perhaps counted on this for, the consulate not having been conferred on him, he now asked Byron for a large loan. When Byron refused he was extremely angry – with his wife. As always, she was equal to his outburst: it had brought about, she said, a relapse which demanded her immediate return to her doctors in Venice. Since she could hardly be expected to undertake such a journey alone, could not Lord Byron accompany her? Thus outmanœuvred, the Count had little option but to agree.

In a sense, this journey took Teresa beyond the limits of acceptable behaviour; to be so blatantly together with her lover threatened the rules of her brittle world, in which everything could be countenanced except the evidence of true emotion. They stayed for a while, struggling to keep up what was left to them of the conventions, in Byron's *palazzo*. They planned to go away together, to Lake Como, and Teresa went so far as to ask her husband's permission to make the journey; even before his reply arrived – he was mysteriously in accord – they had moved to Byron's villa outside Venice, at La Mira. They spent long hours together, happy, loving; in the glow of this joy, Byron worked with gusto at his rumbustious *Don Juan*. Their actual lovemaking may, however, have been somewhat restricted, if the report on her health which Teresa sent her husband is to be believed: she had had, she told him, 'much inconvenience in the last few days from piles', although the doctor had 'reassured me on the point which interested me most, the supposed *prolapsus uteri*. . . .'

A new character now intervened in their dramatic and perhaps over-public idyll: Count Ruggero Gamba, Teresa's father. With affectionate politeness he warned her of the consequences of her present position. 'This most seductive young man is by your side, protecting you – no doubt in a manner honourable and worthy of you both. That may be enough to convince me, and your husband, and your own conscience. But the world will not be satisfied. . . .' Teresa tearfully accepted the snatching away of her tour of the lakes – but remained firmly at La Mira.

Byron meanwhile seems to have become a little restless. He dreamed of projects in Venezuela, even of helping some post-

Peterloo uprising in England. 'Better be an unskilled Planter,' he
wrote to Hobhouse, 'an awkward settler, – better be a hunter, or
anything, than a flatterer of fiddlers, and fan carrier of a woman.'
He may have been more reconciled to his lot by the arrival, early
in October, of Moore. His friend recorded that Byron was fatter,
but 'still, however, eminently handsome'. Byron offered him his
Palazzo Mocenigo and spent his days with him. On his last day in
Venice, Moore visited La Mira and there Teresa saw Byron give
him 'a little bag of paper' – his Memoirs, those famous recollections, so truthful, so candid, so free of cant and thus, in the
gathering fog of puritanism, so incandescently 'indecent', that
after he was dead his friends, gentlemen all and concerned to do
the right, burned them to save his reputation. Better Byron
maligned than Byron truthful.

Byron fell ill with a fever; when he recovered, he found that
Count Guiccioli had at last descended on Venice. While Teresa
would have us believe that all was now sweetness and light, the
truth is that she and her husband quarrelled so bitterly that he
finally forced her to a direct choice between himself and Byron.
'She decided instantly for *me* . . .', Byron wrote, 'the lover
generally having the preference. . . . At twenty I should have
taken her away, at thirty, with the experience of *ten such years*!
I sacrificed myself only. . . .' Teresa's lamentation was great, but
Byron stood firm – it was finally his persuasion that brought her
back to Guiccioli's side. The Count had drawn up a set of 'Indis-

161

pensable Rules' to order her conduct; she wrote a pert set of
'Clauses in Reply to Yours'; Byron had to resolve the deadlock.
Thus Teresa travelled sadly to Ravenna, while Byron prepared to
depart – he wrote to Kinnaird, his agent in London, that 'as I left
England on account of my own wife, I now quit Italy for the wife
of another'.

Yet he did not move. Packed, ready to go, he lingered nevertheless. In fact, he was very reluctant to return to a Britain where the
Edinburgh Magazine had just attacked him as 'an unrepenting,
unsoftened, smiling, sarcastic joyous sinner' for whom there
could be 'neither pity nor pardon'. He must therefore have been
delighted when Count Gamba, unexpectedly convinced that his
daughter would not recover from yet another bout of her endlessly
useful illness unless Byron was at her side, asked him to return to
her. 'I shall go again to Ravenna,' Byron wrote to a friend; 'anything better than England' – though his letter to Teresa was
couched in warmer tones.

In the next few months, although Byron often detested his
enslaved condition – 'I am drilling very hard to learn how to
double a shawl' – and although he was often irritable or suspicious,
he settled fairly easily into a new routine. A little dangerously
installed in the Palazzo Guiccioli, he rode, visited the theatre,
made love when the opportunity offered – and wrote. By mid-
February 1820 he was able to send Murray the second and third
cantos of *Don Juan*. He was at the same time becoming fascinated
by the plots and problems surrounding Italian nationalism,
doubtless because of the many conversations he could now have
with Teresa's father. This, his work, his daughter and his continuing though mellower feeling for Teresa absorbed him. In
that last quarter, however, trouble threatened. Her husband,
having at last rediscovered jealousy, asked Byron to stop seeing
her: he had caught them, Byron wrote to Murray, '*quasi* in the
fact, and, what is worse . . . she did not *deny* it'.

Perhaps because of Byron's political sympathies, perhaps
because of the obvious sincerity of his feelings for Teresa, Count
Gamba had by now taken a great liking to him and with his
support pressure began to be mounted for the Guicciolis' legal
separation, obtainable only by Papal decree. Byron wrote to
Teresa, describing Guiccioli as a man who had 'persecuted you in
words and deeds for injuries to which no one has contributed. . . .
He may abandon you – but I *never*.' He called himself her 'lover,
friend and (when circumstances permit) your *husband*'. Early in

162

Count Pietro Gamba. 'I like your little brother very much,' wrote Byron to Teresa; 'he shows character and talent – Big eyebrows! . . . His head is a little too hot for revolutions – he must not be too rash.'

July, the separation gained papal approval, on the grounds that she could 'no longer live in peace and safety' with her husband. Fighting back, the Count had his eighteen servants sign depositions affirming Teresa's guilt, but by then she had already settled into her father's country house, at Filetto, some fifteen miles from Ravenna.

With some coolness, Byron rejected Guiccioli's demand to quit and remained in the wronged husband's *palazzo*. He was, in fact, quite happy, feeling free, able to work, and engaged in making a new friend – Pietro, Teresa's brother, returned from university in Rome. Pietro was an open-hearted, over-enthusiastic young man, clear-eyed, generous and honest, though with all the hot blood and naïveté of his age and nation. Soon, he and Byron were

163

Count Gamba's villa at Filetto, about fifteen miles from Ravenna.

riding together, shooting, fencing – and planning in an airy way the necessary revolution which would break the power of the papacy and rid the country of the Austrians. Indeed, Byron at this time seems to have joined a secret society, the *Cacciatori Americani*, or American Hunters, a branch of the Ravenna Carbonari. Certainly he was serious enough for the suspicions of the authorities to be aroused.

He installed Allegra in a villa not far from Filetto and thus, in mid-August, he began visiting Teresa again, going first to see his daughter, then journeying on to Filetto. More and more he was becoming attached not only to her, but to all her family. Yet the separation left Teresa dissatisfied; she decided to lessen the distance between them and moved to her father's town house, in Ravenna itself. Despite this, and despite the harassment of the authorities – 'They try to fix squabbles upon my servants, to involve me in scrapes . . . menace to shut Madame Guiccioli up in a *Convent*' – Byron continued to work steadily. By the end of 1820

164

the fifth canto of *Don Juan* had been written. Political action threatened – 'Expect to hear the drum and musket momently,' he wrote in his journal – then, having simmered for a while, cooled – 'Thus the world goes; and thus the Italians are always lost for lack of union among themselves.' Yet the authorities remained active and, early in July 1821, Pietro was banished. Byron was soon convinced that it was he of whom the government wanted to be rid: if Pietro went, so would his father; where the father went, there went Teresa; wherever Teresa was, Byron was at her side. Thus ran official logic, and accurately, too. The Gambas, father, son and daughter, packed up and left Ravenna and the Romagna, seeking asylum elsewhere in Italy. But at that point the logic broke down, for Byron, though constantly on the point of departure, lingered in Ravenna. Not only authority found this irksome; Teresa too complained. Yet Byron's reason was ostensibly good – it was only in Ravenna that he could put pressure on the officials to rescind the Gambas' banishment. With none of his efforts in this direction, however, had he any success.

There is little doubt that he was in many ways quite happy to be alone, genuinely though he missed Teresa and her family. He began a new drama, *Cain*, later to raise horror in pious breasts with its bleak, almost existential view of a world where neither gods nor men can justify themselves and only implacable will opposes a cosmic despair. No wonder that when Shelley arrived to see him on 6 August the two poets sat up talking until five in the morning. Byron, who had hardly spoken with an intellectual equal since Moore's departure, must in this mood have fallen upon the mind of his visitor like a hungry wolf. Shelley found that Byron had 'completely recovered his health', but found his household somewhat bizarre: it consisted, 'besides servants, of ten horses, eight enormous dogs, three monkeys, five cats, an eagle, a crow, and a falcon'. Later, he added that he had 'just met on the grand staircase five peacocks, two guinea hens, and an Egyptian crane'. His opinion of Byron's genius, however, always generously high, remained unchanged. He read three further cantos of *Don Juan* in manuscript: 'I think that every word of it is pregnant with immortality.'

Although Byron had intended to take Teresa and her family, now safely in Florence, to exile in Switzerland, Shelley suggested that instead they should all come to Pisa, where he and Mary were installed. Delighted, Byron wrote to Teresa – Switzerland, he told her, was a country 'where they exile once more those who

165

The Death of Sardanapalus, by Eugène Delacroix, taken from Byron's drama *Sardanapalus*.

Byron's Casa Lanfranchi
at Pisa, a sixteenth-century
palazzo on the bank of
the Arno.

have already been exiled'. Shelley too wrote to her, although at
that time he did not know her, to warn her that Geneva was full of
English people who would certainly persecute both Byron and
her: 'Their admiration for his works is involuntary and they
slander him in consequence of their immoderate prejudices. . . .'
Teresa agreed, being by now almost tetchily impatient to see
Byron again. She wrote to Lega Zambelli, once her husband's
steward, now in Byron's employ, 'Is Mylord pretending? Or does
he really mean to leave Ravenna? Tell me, Lega, I beseech you.'
And to Byron she wrote, 'I vow that if it were allowed me I would
fly to Ravenna. . . . Since I have known you, I have no other
desire than to be where you are – and in your heart.'

Shelley, in the meantime, had found a house for the Gambas in
Pisa and a rambling palace, the Casa Lanfranchi, for Byron.
Everyone waited for Byron to make his journey, yet for some
reason he procrastinated. Weeks passed; the post carried Lega's

168

Lord Clare, a friend of Byron's youth, whom he met again by chance on the road between Imola and Bologna.

endless apologies to Teresa for the delays; surrounded by his packaged goods, increasingly depressed – 'a mountain of lead upon my heart', as he described it – Byron hesitated, waited and, as always, worked. It was at this time that he wrote his brilliant anti-George III, anti-Southey satire, *The Vision of Judgment*.

Late in October 1821 Byron at last left Ravenna, having put Allegra into the convent of Bagnacavallo. It was a journey of meetings, the first a chance encounter with Lord Clare, one of his closest friends at Harrow and in the years immediately after, which seems to have made in its sudden happiness an extraordinary impression on Byron: 'We were but five minutes together, and in the public road; but I hardly recollect an hour of my existence which could be weighed against them.' Travelling on, he stayed in Florence; of his departure there the poet Rogers, who had travelled with him for a while, wrote that 'every window of the inn was open to see him'. There was to be yet one more

169

Edward John Trelawny.
After Byron first met him he
told Teresa: 'I have met
today the personification of
my Corsair.'

brush with the past on the journey; near Empoli, Byron passed
the public coach. Unseen among its passengers, Claire Clairmont
looked eagerly out, recognising Byron's great Napoleonic
vehicle, her heart doubtless leaping with the abruptness of that
sight, perhaps restraining herself from leaning out, giving a cry,
making a gesture, before Byron, relentless, unaware, eyes on a
different future, had whirled for the last time out of her sight.

'I have got here into a famous old feudal palazzo, on the
Arno,' Byron wrote to Murray from Pisa. He had a garden, too,
orange trees in it, and the climate of a sheltered town to keep him
warm. More importantly, he had now a circle of English friends,
introduced to him by Shelley. One of them, Edward Williams,
wrote of Byron, 'So far from his having haughtiness of manner,
they are those of the most unaffected and gentlemanly ease . . . he
is all sunshine and good humour. . . .' Apart from Williams and his

170

wife – she had been the wife of one of Williams's brother officers, but they had eloped – there was Medwin, Shelley's cousin, and Taaffe, an Irishman who had been obliged to travel as a result of an amatory entanglement in Scotland. There was, later, Trelawny, tall, bearded, over-boisterous, with pretensions to being a traveller and adventurer, a man who could never entirely resist the temptation to re-invent his own life or the lives of others. And there was Mary Shelley, friendly to Byron, yet never quite without suspicions – though whether of him or herself is not always absolutely clear.

By the end of the year, dinner at the Casa Lanfranchi was a weekly affair for the men of this group, happy, excited evenings during which the talk leaped and frolicked, speculative, scurrilous, philosophical, blasphemous, literary, political and obscene by turns. One visitor almost certainly brought to life feelings now long dormant in Byron, with consequences unguessable, yet rapidly approaching: the exiled Greek patriot, Prince Argiropoli.

Medwin has given us a portrait of Byron as he appeared on those evenings, commenting on his generous courtesy, rare in the fluent talker – 'He gives everyone an opportunity of sharing in the conversation, and has the art of turning it to subjects that may bring out the person with whom he converses . . . his anecdotes of life and living characters is inexhaustable. In spirits, as in every thing else, he is ever in extremes.' Byron, it is clear, was content with his much fuller life in Pisa. His poetic stock in London still stood high, with Murray advancing him 2500 guineas for the new cantos of *Don Juan* and his dramas, including *Cain*. Only Teresa was doubtful, feeling that Byron was growing away from her – natural enough, perhaps, after so long a period during which she and her family had been the only people with whom he had felt truly at ease.

In England, Annabella's mother, Lady Noel (the family had changed its name to conform to the conditions of a will) died at the end of January. Rather sentimentally, perhaps, Byron told Medwin of his distress for Annabella: 'She must be in great affliction, for she adored her mother!' He too added 'Noel' to his name and thus became the recipient of another £2500 a year, bringing his income to over £6000 a year, vast for the times. But his life, though pleasant, was far from untroubled: there were rumours that Murray would be prosecuted for bringing out *Cain*, Claire was agitating for the return of her daughter from the convent, Teresa was at times discontented, at others jealous.

171

Now, in mid-March, a slightly ridiculous quarrel with a soldier – he had galloped past the party as they were riding and frightened Taaffe's horse – led to a fracas near the city gate in which Shelley fell from his horse and another of the party had his nose cut. The matter became truly serious only when the soldier, turning away either in fear or fury, and galloping past Byron's Casa Lanfranchi, was stabbed by someone who immediately ran away through the crowd. Two of Byron's servants were arrested on suspicion; the wrong one, Tita, paid the penalty for his ferocious appearance – great size, great beard, brace of pistols – and was kept in prison. As if this incident had been a signal marking the intrusion of a sour, external world into their hitherto delightful, closed one, the group began to break up. It had almost dwindled away by the time Byron was installed in his summer villa near Leghorn.

By then, however, Byron must have felt that he needed those months of planned recuperation and quiet which now apparently stretched ahead. For early in April he had heard from Bagnacavallo that Allegra was ill with a slight fever. She had been better by the middle of the month, then had had a slight relapse; abruptly, on 20 April, she had died 'after a convulsive catarrhal attack'. It was Teresa who had had to tell Byron: 'A mortal paleness spread itself over his face', yet 'he did not shed a tear. . . . He remained immovable in the same attitude for an hour, and no consolation which I endeavoured to afford him seemed to reach his ears. . . .' But Byron had not gone to Bagnacavallo, he had refused to receive messengers from the convent, he had ceased altogether to speak of the dead child. It was as if he could not bear to reveal feelings imposed on him by outside events, could not afford the slightest loss of control. (One is forced to recall that he did not follow his mother's funeral procession, sparring with Rushton as usual that day – until after all unable to continue.) Over Allegra, he seems, however, to have felt some guilt; he wrote to Shelley, 'I do not know that I have anything to reproach in my conduct, and certainly nothing in my feelings and intentions towards the dead. But it is a moment when we are apt to think that, if this or that had been done, such event might have been prevented.'

As a result, Byron had sunk into one of his recurrent melancholies; Pisa, he must have realised, had ceased to be any long-term refuge for him and the Gambas. Although the case against Tita had ended in the man's being shorn and banished, beardless

A scene from Byron's drama
The Two Foscari, by Eugène
Delacroix.

174

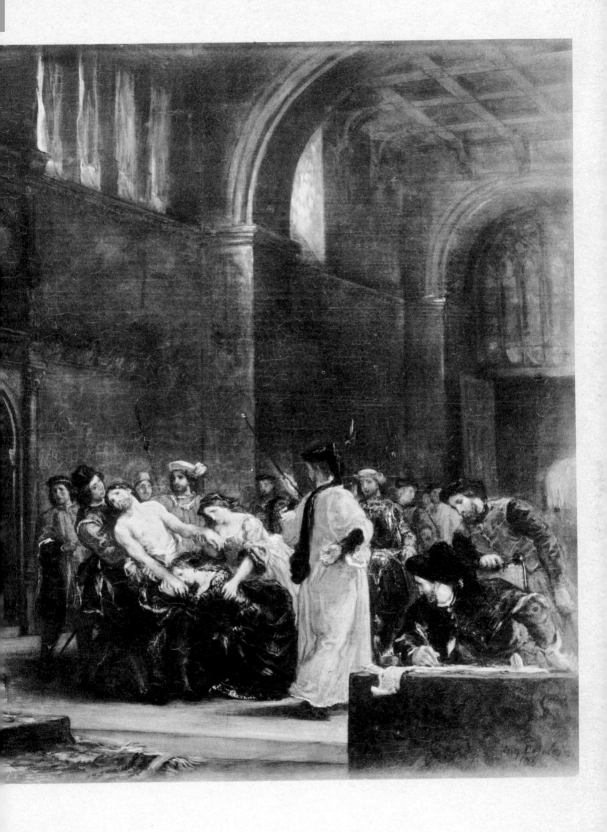

The Casa Magni, Shelley's
house near Lerici.

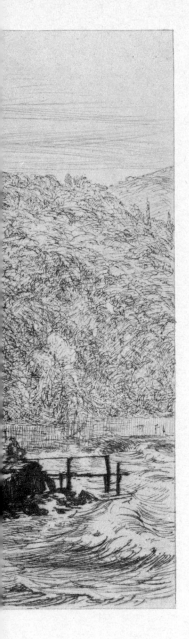

(to appear shortly afterwards at the Casa Magni, the Shelleys' summer home near Lerici), the authorities were restive and plainly anxious for these dangerous trouble-makers to be gone. Yet Byron had lingered in Pisa, as he had earlier in Ravenna, apparently unable to move. But with what was later to become known as the 'Pisan Circle' broken up for ever, he had finally moved to the low, rambling house he had taken as a summer residence, the Villa Dupuy.

Here, he might have spent the long, hot months, happy at last in the now-domestic delights of Teresa's company, enjoying the tranquillity of his garden, walking there with her, watching in the ship-littered bay below the comings and goings of the port of Leghorn. Instead, another minor incident seems to have been the trigger which finally activated the dislike of the authorities. Pietro Gamba, intervening in a servants' quarrel, was stabbed in the arm by the excitable coachman, Papi. Leigh Hunt, arriving at that moment on a visit largely paid for through Byron's generosity, stepped into the middle of melodrama – 'I fancied myself pitched into one of the scenes in the *Mysteries of Udolpho*.' He found that, 'though the stab was not much, the inflictor of it threatened more', besieging the house, 'his eye glaring upwards like a tiger'. But when Byron, 'composed and endeavouring to compose', went out to him, Papi, suddenly overwhelmed with remorse, flung himself down, asked forgiveness and demanded that Byron kiss him. 'The noble lord conceived such an excess of charity superfluous,' Hunt records. Though making fun of the incident, Hunt saw that for Byron 'it increased the awkwardness of his position with the Tuscan Government. . . . His friends, the Gambas, were already only upon sufferance in Tuscany.' Thus the peace of Byron's summer abruptly collapsed. The Gambas were summoned to a tribunal and ordered to leave the country within three days (though this was later extended). Byron wrote to the Governor of Leghorn, 'I will not remain any longer in a place where my friends are persecuted, and a refuge is denied to the unfortunate.'

He returned to Pisa, knowing now that he was unlikely to remain there long. It was the considerate Shelley who shepherded the Hunts to the Casa Lanfranchi and saw them settled into their prepared apartment there, Shelley who persuaded Byron to assign first publication of *The Vision of Judgment* to the journal Hunt was in the process of founding. Only then did he return to Leghorn, where Williams was waiting with their boat, ready to

sail back to Lerici. Byron, harassed by the almost certain prospect of soon moving again, now saw Leigh Hunt and his family as little more than a collective nuisance. And Mrs Hunt almost at once took up an attitude of middle-class outrage at Byron's relationship with Teresa. She must have seemed to Byron, surrounded as she was by virtue and a clutch of sticky children, the epitomy of that sour censoriousness he had been faced with all his life.

The Gambas had come to rest, at least for a while, in Lucca; Teresa settled snugly into the Casa Lanfranchi, for the first time openly in her lover's care; a new routine began to make orderly, as always, Byron's life. It was soon to be cruelly disturbed. On the night after Shelley's departure for Lerici, Leigh Hunt recalls, 'there was a tremendous storm of thunder and lightning, which made us very anxious; but we hoped our friend had arrived before then'. But on 10 July Trelawny arrived in Pisa. He had seen Shelley's boat, the *Don Juan*, ten miles off Viareggio; the storm had

OPPOSITE Leigh Hunt. 'He is a good man, with some poetical elements in his chaos, but spoilt by the Christ-Church Hospital and a Sunday newspaper, – to say nothing of the Surrey goal, which conceived him into a martyr.'

LEFT The *Don Juan* and the *Bolivar*, sketched by Edward Williams.

179

come down, darkly bombarding the sea, then risen, cleared; the boat had vanished. Hunt wrote to Shelley at the Casa Magni; on the 13th, Mary Shelley, 'as white as marble', Teresa remembered, arrived at Byron's door: '*Sapete alcuna cosa di Shelley*?' But there was nothing further now that would ever be known about Shelley; from this moment, only his reputation would grow and alter as though alive. Leigh Hunt records, 'A dreadful interval took place of more than a week. . . . At the end of that period, our worst fears were confirmed. A body had been washed on shore, near the town of Via Reggio [sic], which by the dress and stature, was known to be our friend's.' A copy of Keats in the jacket pocket helped in the identification: 'It was my copy. I had told him to keep it till he gave it me with his own hands. . . . It was burnt with his remains.'

Byron was among the few who understood the value, private and public, of the drowned poet. He was, he told Murray, 'the *best* and least selfish man I ever knew. I never knew one who was not a beast in comparison.' To Moore he was perhaps more bitter – 'There is thus another mañ gone, about whom the world was ill-naturedly, and ignorantly, and brutally mistaken.' It was Trelawny who organised the almost pagan funerals held on the beach, the bodies of the two men being burned on successive days. According to him, Byron looked at the remains of Williams and said, 'Are we to resemble that? – why it might be the carcase of a sheep for all I can see.' He swam out to sea, becoming ill a mile from the shore and having to struggle back. On the next day, 19 August 1822, the body of Shelley was laid on its pyre, Trelawny going so far as to utter incantations over the flames. Hunt remained in his carriage, overcome, and Byron did not stay long, but wandered away, alone at the edge of the sea.

Yet despite his distress, despite the Hunts and their persistent and undisciplined brood of six – 'Hunt's theory and practice were that children should be unrestrained until they were of an age to be reasoned with,' Trelawny tells us – Byron continued to work on *Don Juan*. Teresa, who had forbidden him to add to the poem when she read it in a French translation, had now lifted her prohibition and, by the end of August, three more cantos had been written. Time was also taken up with the planning of Hunt's journal, to be named *The Liberal*, for which Hunt thought the support and partnership of Byron essential. Thus occupied, the household seemed once more busy and at peace; yet it was in its last weeks.

The Gambas had now been promised asylum in Genoa, had taken a house there and were waiting for Byron and Teresa to join them. However, before Byron could make the move, Hobhouse appeared on a visit to Pisa. Teresa recorded that Byron was with her in the garden when Hobhouse was announced: 'The slight shade of melancholy on Lord Byron's face gave instant place to the liveliest joy. . . . A fearful paleness came over his cheeks, and his eyes were filled with tears, as he embraced his friend.' Hobhouse found Byron 'much changed – his face fatter, and the expression of it injured'. He disapproved of his friend's political involvements, and was fairly scornful of his relationship with Teresa and of the Gambas, finding her family's tolerance of Byron disgraceful – 'This is Italian morality.' As a politician, he had perhaps had to learn the language of humbug. He remained for a little while, though perhaps the old familiarity was not easily arrived at now between these two men, always so different in essence and parted for so long. However, Hobhouse's departure moved them both. Byron said to him, 'Hobhouse, you should never have come, or you should never go.'

On 28 September Byron, Teresa, Trelawny and the Hunts left Pisa for the last time. Torelli, a spy and tool of the Austrians, recorded their going: 'Mylord has at length decided to leave for Genoa. It is said that he is already tired of his new favourite, the Guiccioli. He has expressed his intention of not remaining in Genoa, but of going on to Athens to purchase adoration from the Greeks.'

Settled in Genoa, in the Casa Saluzzo, he, Teresa, the Gambas and three large geese under its four-square roof, Byron energetically tackled the tenth and eleventh cantos of *Don Juan*. At the same time, he was saving money, his mind once more on the Levant. That may not, however, have been the only reason – he wrote to his agent, Kinnaird, just before his thirty-fifth birthday, that 'now the *dross* is coming, and I *loves lucre*. For we must love something'. And then he added, as he so often does, a remark which seems to hint at an inner emptiness: 'At any rate, then, I have a passion the more, and thus a feeling.' Yet he had visions of action, of travel, of faraway places. Trelawny noted: 'He exhausted himself in planning, projecting, beginning, wishing, intending, postponing, regretting, and doing nothing.' It did not help that he was dieting again. Leigh Hunt continued to irritate him, too, with his obsequious arrogance and his manner of aggressive begging – 'I will trouble you for another "cool

The Countess of Blessington. 'Miladi seems highly literary. . . . She is also very pretty, even in the morning, – a species of beauty on which the sun of Italy does not shine so frequently as the Chandelier.'

hundred" of your crowns.' Byron also tried to help Mary Shelley, but she was prickly, put on her guard by Hunt's gossip.

Byron had by now, it seems, also drifted some distance from Teresa; sometimes whole days would pass without their meeting and they would communicate only by notes. They rode together, sometimes, and went for walks; in the nights, as always, Byron worked. Outside observers were amazed at what they saw as the tedium of the household. One may wonder how Byron stood it; but he had his poetry and his plans. It was perhaps harder for Teresa, who had only Byron. She was not yet twenty-four, and had been exposed to the exuberant glitter of Italian high society for a tantalisingly short while. At the same time, she sensed Byron's increasing restlessness; this is clear from her reaction when, one day, he asked her to sit for a miniature: 'She could only answer him with tears,' she wrote in her third-person *Vie de Lord Byron*. She knew he was thinking of mementoes of partings and distance. She did not know that emissaries from the Greek Committee, a group of men resident in London but dedicated to the cause of Greek freedom, were already planning to visit him.

In April there arrived, disturbing this stagnation, a luminary of the London social scene, Lady Blessington. She, literally sold into marriage when fifteen, had used her gifts of character, beauty and intelligence to struggle to metropolitan leadership, marrying Lord Blessington on the way. With her, apart from her husband, came the young exquisite, the Count D'Orsay, and there is a piquancy in imagining his meeting with Byron, these two cool wits sizing each other up, dandies and social enchanters of different generations. Lady Blessington described the Byron she met; she sounds disappointed because he did not 'look like my preconceived notion of the melancholy poet. . . . His hair has already much of silver among its dark brown curls; its texture is very silky, and although it retreats from his temples, leaving his forehead very bare, its growth at the sides and back of his head is abundant . . . there is something so striking in his whole appearance, that could not be mistaken for an ordinary person. . . .' Only his own awareness of it made her aware of his limp; she thought his voice had an accent 'particularly clear and harmonious, but somewhat effeminate. . . .'

Byron took to the Blessingtons with zest; he rode with Lady Blessington almost every day, spent many evenings in conversation with her and those around her. Teresa, already upset by the hints Byron had given her of his desire to depart, became predictably jealous. 'La mia dama', Byron wrote, '. . . was as unreasonable and perverse as can well be imagined' – yet for no reason, for he 'would much rather fall into the sea than in love, any day of the week'. Certainly Lady Blessington considered his relationship with Teresa permanent – 'I am persuaded this is his last attachment.' In any case, at the end of May, this source of discord vanished as the Blessington party travelled on to Naples and the South; by then, Byron himself was already deep in the preparations for his expedition to Greece. He had been visited by Edward Blaquiere, of the London Greek Committee, and Andreas Luriottis, representing the new and hopefully independent Government of Greece; they had asked him to help in the struggle against Turkish domination and he had agreed.

He had been too soft-hearted to speak directly to Teresa of his intentions, and had asked her brother Pietro to intercede. Teresa wrote of her reaction to the news, 'To her a death sentence would have seemed less terrible.' In the weeks that followed, she sent Byron desperate notes and wept whenever they met. Byron wrote to Kinnaird, 'I am doing all I can to get away, but I have all

OPPOSITE TOP A view of Venice, by J.M.W.Turner. BOTTOM Byron in the Palazzo Mocenigo, by J.S.Davis.

RIGHT Byron wearing the Homeric helmet he ordered specially for his Greek adventure.

BELOW The helmet – now at Newstead Abbey – with the Byron coat of arms and the motto 'Crede Byron'.

kinds of obstacles thrown in my way by "the absurd woman-kind". . . .' Yet his own mood was mixed, enthusiasm alternating with self-mockery. As he said to Lady Blessington, he found himself at times absurd in his enthusiasms, 'fit only for a travestie'. At the same time, however, he felt that he would die in Greece, and one does not know whether this is the last echo of Childe Harold's voice, a genuine presentiment or possibly even a wish. According to Lady Blessington, Byron 'had a conviction that he should never return from Greece. He had dreamt more than once, he assured me, of dying there.' He hoped it would be in action – 'I have a horror of death-bed scenes,' he said.

Nevertheless, helped by Trelawny and Pietro Gamba, who had agreed to travel with him, he prepared energetically: medical supplies were purchased, a doctor engaged, a ship, the *Hercules*, chartered, splendid uniforms prepared – and, absurdly perhaps, three helmets ordered, his own heroic, classical, with a great plume, Trelawny's similar, Pietro's decorated with a figure of Athena. Kinnaird gave him a letter of credit for £4000; he already had £2000 in Italy. Wolf-like, the Greeks in Genoa slipped on patriotism like sheep's clothing; they saw Byron and his money as a means to cushion exile. The predatory display which followed should have hardened him for what was to come.

For Teresa, the last days and hours must have been intolerable. In a way, she knew herself to be helpless. That Byron wanted to leave at all must have seemed to her the mark of her failure. She wanted to wait in Genoa until he returned, but her father had been given back his passport and wished only to go home to Ravenna as soon as possible. Yet she, like Byron himself, felt that she would never see him again, although it was his intention to do no more than examine the Greek situation and assess what might best be done. She noticed, and later recalled for Moore, that Byron was less determined to leave than he might have admitted: 'Every person who was near him at that time, can bear witness to the struggle his heart underwent (however much he endeavoured to hide it) as the period fixed for his departure approached.' But he had to go – it was as if poetry, domesticity, sexual adventure had all ceased to stimulate. Only direct action and the chance of death remained. For if he did not feel, he did not feel he lived.

'The fateful day arrived at last' – thus Teresa, remembering herself on that 13 July (strange day for a superstitious man to have chosen), sitting on the terrace beside Mary Shelley, seeing far below the *Hercules*, Byron already on board. 'From 3 to 5 he

Pray Jerome is his
Lordship writing that
note for me.
No Sir he is writing
Poetry —
How do you know that
Because he is scratch-
ing his head

Pub.d Jan.y 1, 1823 by J. Johnston 98 Cheapside.   L.d Byron.

A NOBLE POET — Scratching up his Ideas.

1 Jan.y 1923

stayed with Madame Guiccioli,' she writes, those two numbers enclosing the last hours in which she ever saw him. Next morning, pale, stumbling as though drugged, she was to be led to her father's coach. Halted at midday because she felt so ill, she struggled to express her feelings: 'I have promised more than I can perform, and you have asked of me what is beyond my strength. . . . I feel as if I were dying, Byron, have pity on me. . . .' It was a note she never sent, imagining Byron by then on his ship, sails set, forging south-eastward.

The reality was slightly different, as though Byron were matching her sublime despair with his own ridiculous misfortunes. First a calm held the *Hercules* for two days; a tow by the American Navy took them out to sea, where the wind blew so strongly by contrast that it terrified the horses and made Pietro very sea-sick. On the 16th, therefore, with the *Hercules* back in harbour, Byron and Pietro, already ghosts from a dead past, wandered for the last time through the empty rooms of the Casa Saluzzo. Five days later, they were safely in Leghorn – Byron, Pietro wrote to his sister, was 'very much occupied, and happy in his occupations'. Here Byron took on two more companions, Vitali, a Greek captain, and a Scotsman, James Hamilton Browne. On 24 July the *Hercules* left harbour, heading south-east for the Straits of Messina, bound eastward from there, for the Ionian Islands.

OPPOSITE *A noble poet scratching up ideas.* A caricature of Byron writing *Don Juan.*

LEFT A drawing of Byron by Count d'Orsay, before his departure for Greece. 'I have a request to make to my friend Alfred,' wrote Byron to Lady Blessington, '. . . that he would condescend to add a cap to the gentleman in the jacket – it would complete the costume – & smooth his brow which is somewhat too *inveterate* a likeness of the original, God help me!'

6 Death

My task is done, my song hath ceased, my theme
Has died into an echo; it is fit
The spell should break of this protracted dream.
The torch shall be extinguish'd which hath lit
My midnight lamp – and what is writ, is writ . . .

'I DON'T KNOW WHY IT IS, but I feel as if the eleven long years of bitterness I have passed through since I was here, were taken off my shoulders. . . .' Thus Byron, seeing again from the deck of the *Hercules* the far-away mountains of the Morea. He was on his way to Cephalonia, in the British-protected 'United States' of the Ionian Islands. Governed by 'King Tom of Corfu', Sir Thomas Maitland, these islands were neutral in the struggle against the Turks, to the fury of the Greeks and their supporters, who could see their strategic potential without being able to make use of it. As a British visitor, and a famous one, Byron was made welcome, despite his clear intention of helping Greece toward independence.

On the mainland, meanwhile, the nationalist movement was splintering into factions; its story seemed for the moment to consist of dissension, defeat, stalemate, threat or flight. There were, however, several leaders of honour, ability and stature in the Greek forces; Byron wrote for news to one of these, Marco Botsaris, who commanded north of Missolonghi, then settled down with unaccustomed patience to wait for a reply. With a party of friends, he visited the nearby island of Ithaca, and the consequent journeys on muleback and excursions through a minor wilderness of mountains brought back to him exhilarating echoes of his youth, though he seems to have been ill for some of the time. A traveller who had joined the party recalled that on one occasion Byron 'looked like a man under sentence of death. . . . His person seemed shrunk, his face was pale, and his eyes languid and fixed on the ground.'

After four days spent on Ithaca, they returned to Cephalonia. A reply at last arrived from Botsaris: 'Let nothing prevent you from coming. . . . the enemy threatens us in great number; but, by the help of God and your Excellency, they shall meet a suitable resistance.' Within days, however, Botsaris was dead. Byron, uncertain as a consequence of what he should do next and anxious to get the facts about the situation on the mainland, was bombarded with petitions, demands, promises and schemes by practically every Greek who could plausibly present himself as a patriot. An observer, himself come to assist the Greek cause, wrote later: 'Almost every distinguished statesman and general sent him letters soliciting his favour, his influence or his money.' Byron, who understood the weaknesses of the Greek character as well as he did the strength of the Greek cause, proved surprisingly tolerant, and surprisingly patient. What he wanted to see before he made any real move was the emergence of a unified

PREVIOUS PAGES *Lord Byron's Dream,* by Sir Charles Eastlake.
*The Mountains look
        on Marathon –
And Marathon looks
        on the sea;
And musing there an
        hour alone,
I dream'd that Greece
        might still be free . . .*

OPPOSITE Marco Botsaris, the Suliot leader.

192

coalition among the nationalist factions.

In the meantime, the Suliote guard he had hired proved increasingly restive and difficult, and he paid them off. Trelawny, impatient by temperament and long determined to find himself a place in the struggle somewhat out of Byron's enormous shadow, set off for the mainland, accompanied by Browne, the Scotsman. Byron himself, with Pietro and Dr Bruno in attendance, moved to a small, four-roomed villa, little more than a cottage, in the village of Metaxata. From there, he wrote to Teresa, 'I shall fulfill the object of my mission from the committee – and then (probably) return to Italy for it does not seem likely that as an individual I can be of use to them. . . . Pray be as cheerful and tranquil as you can – and be assured that there is nothing here that can excite anything but a wish to be with you again. . . .' Like his other letters to her from Greece, it was flat and dutiful, rather than passionate.

Through weary weeks, while advice and information reached him in complex and contradictory streams, Byron waited on Cephalonia. He wanted to form a corps with which to fight on the mainland, but could not see how such a force could be used to the best advantage. In the meantime he helped in the raising of the funds necessary to put the Greeks' small navy on a respectable war footing, making a personal loan for that purpose of £4000. In November, however, he received a message from the nationalist Senate, then at Salamis: 'Now it has been considered necessary that there should be sent to Missolonghi, for the direction of affairs in that locality and of whole Western Greece, that good patriot and president of the Legislative Party, Alexander Mavrocordato, Your Excellency is begged to help spontaneously, in any way you think best, at Missolonghi. . . .' This town, Missolonghi, which Byron had briefly glimpsed fourteen years before, was considered an essential base for any attack on Patras and Lepanto, the last surviving Turkish strongholds on the mainland. For that reason, it was not only a springboard for further advance, but also a bulwark which had to be defended against the Turkish offensive expected the following spring.

Mavrocordato landed there on 11 December. From his new headquarters, he sent a series of letters to Byron. He also sent ships to carry him back to Missolonghi, but these, because of the strict neutrality maintained by the British controlling the islands, were not allowed to land. To Mavrocordato's frustration, therefore, they returned each time without Byron. His letters became more urgent: 'My Lord, Here is a third letter. . . . As I have

OPPOSITE Alexander Mavrocordato, the Greek patriot, and president of the Legislative Party, wrote to Byron: 'Your presence will do the greatest good: our forces will be electrified; the enthusiasm of all will be kindled. . . .'

195

written already, I should never . . . have accepted a task whose magnitude and difficulty I foresaw, had I not counted upon the co-operation of Your Excellency. . . . Your presence will do the greatest good: our forces will be electrified; the enthusiasm of all will be kindled. . . .'

Byron, at last accepting that the coalition he wanted would not come into existence either easily or soon, and convinced that Mavrocordato represented an authority as nearly legitimate as the Greeks could muster, decided to leave Metaxata. He hired two local boats, perhaps in order to make use of their neutral flags, and set off for Missolonghi on 29 December. Pietro Gamba was with him, Fletcher, his old servant, Dr Bruno, Lega Zambelli, a cluster of other servants, Lion, his Newfoundland dog, the bulldog, Moretto – and, echo of his previous stay in the Eastern Mediterranean, Loukas Chalandritsanos, a good-looking fifteen-year-old boy whom he had taken under his protection.

The crossing to the mainland proved more adventurous than Byron might have hoped. His two ships soon lost sight of each other; the last glimpse he had of Pietro's vessel was as it disappeared into the dawn, pursued by a Turkish warship. Themselves creeping past a watching Turkish patrol, Byron and his companions put into a safe harbour and sent for help from Mavrocordato. Even when an escort arrived from Missolonghi, however, high winds made the return journey both dangerous and prolonged. Pietro's ship, meanwhile, was actually in Turkish hands when their captors' commander recognised in his Greek opposite number the man who had once saved his life. Although the ship was taken into Patras, Pietro and the others were treated with great courtesy and soon allowed to leave. Pietro was clearly surprised to discover that despite all these vicissitudes, he was at Missolonghi before Byron.

The village of Missolonghi stands, trapped in its own dank swamps, a little way inland from the Gulf of Patras. The occasional long swell on the dark waters of its neighbouring lagoon does nothing to dispel the sense of dangerous stagnation, of earth and water settled into sullen putrefaction, which seems to oppress all those who visit it. Yet it was never nearer being overwhelmed by excitement than when, on the morning of 5 January 1824, Byron, dressed in a brilliant red uniform, stepped ashore there to wild applause and the enthusiastic welcome of Mavrocordato and the other Greek leaders. 'Lord Byron has been received like a delivering Angel,' Pietro Gamba wrote to his sister. 'Affairs here are

OPPOSITE A scene from Byron's *Don Juan*, by Charles Rickett.

196

going better and better . . . and the Greeks all turn to Byron for the composition of all their discussions, which are now completely resolved.' It is a pity that history so rarely answered Pietro's optimistic expectations of it.

There were now some five thousand soldiers in Missolonghi, turning its dingy houses and miasmic swamps into an unlikely background for their colourful belligerence. Lepanto was their immediate goal, and Mavrocordato offered Byron a force to lead in the projected attack. Byron agreed to pay for five hundred soldiers; another hundred were added to his detachment, at government expense. He now had what he had perhaps often dreamed of – his own private army of Suliotes, exiled warriors from the mountains of Albania. An observer remarked, 'His house was filled with soldiers; his receiving room resembled an arsenal of war . . . and attacks, surprises, charges, ambuscades, battles, sieges, were almost the only topics of his conversation with the different capitani.'

Byron helped in the founding of an artillery detachment, essential to an effective siege, and paid £100 towards the cost of it. On the open space behind the house he shared with other foreigners, beside the dark and sluggish waters of the lagoon, he drilled his Suliotes; off duty, they were quartered in the out-buildings or the damp ground floor. The nationalist government, both the legislative and the executive branches, wrote and asked for his help in raising yet another loan in London; as if in part-payment, they apologised for their own dissensions.

Byron, however, had dissension enough on his own doorstep. The townsfolk were becoming increasingly disillusioned with the high-handed and largely penniless soldiery, many of whom behaved very like brigands. On 18 January this ill-feeling erupted into a dialogue of musketry. A Suliote had moved into a house while the owner was temporarily away; the householder, returned, had complained to someone, standing in the street and voicing his disgust. The Suliote, passing by, had shot him dead. Eventually, the quarrelling and its attendant shooting died away, but within the hour there came the more serious news that the Turkish fleet had sailed out of Patras harbour. The five ships guarding Missolonghi fled, exposing the town to blockade. This made the expected arrival of men and equipment for the artillery unit hazardous, if not impossible.

For Byron, these public frustrations were joined with one more private. It was at this time that he wrote one of his last poems.

198

L. Dupré

T'is time this heart should be unmoved,
Since others it hath ceased to move:
Yet though I cannot be beloved,
   Still let me love!

My days are in the yellow leaf;
The flowers and fruits of Love are gone;
The worm, the canker, and the grief
   Are mine alone!

OPPOSITE *The Massacres of Scio*, by Eugène Delacroix, a bloody episode in the Greek War of Independence.

These verses, the beginning of a poem whose later lines are more often quoted – 'The Sword, the Banner, and the Field, Glory and Greece, around me see!' – was wrung from him by the indifference of Loukas, his page boy and the last of his loves. For years he had proclaimed his physical decay and one feels that this, like so much else in his life, was an effort to control even the uncontrollable. By defining something, by being the first to point it out, by meeting or even by falsifying it, Byron had always attempted to conquer the inevitable. He had often imitated love, as if to avoid becoming its victim. He had accepted his alienation from the ordinary by emphasising it, transmuting lameness into arrogance. He had quenched grief, while allowing himself a contrived and extravagant despair. Yet under all his masks, a real face lived – and altered. Again and again reality had outmanœuvred him, as it always must; now it had done so once more. Loukas, disdaining Byron as a lover, accepted with arrogant ingratitude his benefactions. What attention, what appearances of affection, Byron received from him, he had to buy.

The weariness and melancholy this raised in Byron was not counterweighted by any successes in the cause he had so enthusiastically taken up. Despite the wealth of some of the Greek leaders, not one seemed able to help him in financing the forces of liberation. His five hundred Suliotes had brought with them another seven hundred dependants and expected him to provide for them all. But when supplies arrived, these proud mountain people refused to demean themselves by carrying them up the beach. When William Parry, the firemaster in charge of the artillery equipment, finally reached Missolonghi, prepared to take charge of the unit, he found that there was hardly any money for his work – and Byron, as usual, supplied the deficiency. Indeed, it began to seem more and more as though he alone was expected to finance the attack on Lepanto. Parry soon sensed 'that he felt himself deceived and abandoned, I had almost said

201

Byron's house at
Missolonghi.

Byron and his dog Lion, with Byron's Suliote guards in
the background.

204

betrayed . . . in his heart, he felt that he was forlorn and forsaken'.

His Suliotes, quarrelsome and as concerned with punctilio, honour and precedence as a courtful of diplomats, bickered endlessly and violently among themselves, unwilling to take orders from or even co-operate with each other. Most of them wanted to be officers; Pietro Gamba reported that 'out of three or four hundred actual Suliotes, there should be about one hundred and fifty above the rank of common soldiers. Their object, of course, was to increase their pay.' Byron refused to have any more to do with them. 'They may go to the Turks, or the Devil. . . .' he wrote to Mavrocordato. Faced with the sudden termination of their relative wealth, the Suliotes agreed to form a more orderly troop.

The strain had, however, overtaxed Byron's strength. On 15 February he had a kind of fit. 'He foamed at the mouth, gnashed his teeth, and rolled his eyes like one in an epilepsy,' Dr Millingen, recently sent out from England, noted at the time. When Pietro Gamba arrived, Byron asked him if he was dying: 'Let me know. Do not think I am afraid to die – I am not.'

Next day, despite Byron's protests, he was bled; once begun, however, the bleeding could not be stopped until nearly midnight. Yet even when as weak as he was the following day, he retained his magnanimity, trying to ensure the safety of a number of captured Turkish women. Two days later, there was another violent dispute in which a Suliote was wounded; a rumour that a foreigner had killed him (in fact it was a Swiss, Captain Sass, who had been killed) brought a furious crowd to Byron's house, raucously threatening to kill the foreigners living there. Byron drew up cannon, prepared for effective defence; when, partly as a result, the immediate excitement had subsided, he summoned the Suliote leaders. 'Facing the mutinous Suliots, covered with dirt and splendid attires,' an eye-witness recorded, Byron was 'electrified'; he 'seemed to recover from his sickness; and the more the Suliots raged, the more his calm courage triumphed'.

Byron improved during the next few days. 'This attack,' Pietro wrote to his sister, 'has brought him to his senses and the good it has done has been to make him change his way of life entirely.' In a postscript, Byron added, 'We are all very well *now* – and everything appears to wear a hopeful aspect.' But he was neither really well, nor in any true sense optimistic. His Suliotes had decided that the proposed attack on Lepanto did not really appeal to them. 'They owned that they did not like to fight against stone walls,' Pietro recorded. 'Lord Byron offered to give them a month's pay if they would go. . . .' Then, on Saturday, 21 February, an earthquake shook the little town; superstitiously, 'the whole army discharged their arms', Byron noted drily, 'upon the same principle that savages beat drums, or howl, during an eclipse. . . .' But despite these revivals of his caustic wit, he felt that he had come to the end of his hopes: 'In one week I have been in a fit; the troops mutinied . . . Sass killed; an earthquake; thunder, lightning, and torrents of rain – such a week I never witnessed.' He said this to Parry; to others he observed, 'My situation here is unbearable. A town without any resources and a Government without money; imprisoned by the floods, unable to take any exercise, without the means of . . . doing anything either to relieve them or myself.'

Yet, tantalisingly, there were signs that success was close, or at least achievable. The Albanians who largely garrisoned Lepanto had dropped the price of their surrender from an original 40,000 dollars to 25,000 dollars. (Even so, the Suliotes refused to move.) And a message arrived from Odysseus, one of the most prominent and devious of Greek leaders still following an independent line, asking Byron and Mavrocordato to a meeting in Salona. Despite doubts about trusting him, the offer suggested that Greek unity was becoming possible, especially if Byron remained its focus; he was even offered the Governor-Generalship of the new Greece by the government, now meeting in Kranidi.

Yet all the old problems remained. On 25 March, Mavrocordato wrote to Byron, 'The till is not only empty, but in debt as well.' And three days later, one of the artillerymen robbed a local peasant and had to be punished. These difficulties left their mark on Byron and Parry wrote, 'As his hopes of the cause of Greece failed . . . he became peevish. . . . There was no mental stimulus left to make him bear up against his increasing perplexities. . . .' He even quarrelled with Pietro Gamba, over an order for red cloth which Byron thought excessive.

The date set for the Salona conference came and went; impassable roads and swollen rivers in that low-lying and rain-soaked place kept Byron in Missolonghi. March ground towards April, and still the rain fell, grey sky to grey water. Byron had written to Teresa – the last letter he was ever to send her – 'The Spring is come – I have seen a Swallow today. . . . We are all very well, which will I hope – keep up your hopes and Spirits.' Now, weeks after this dispirited piece of routine optimism, Pietro wrote,

206

Odysseus, one of the most popular heroes of the Greek
war, and later governor-general of eastern Greece, was
nevertheless, when Byron had to deal with him, devious
and unreliable.

'Fifteen days ago we promised to go to Salona . . . but the un-
favourable weather and the impossible roads have kept us here
until now . . . Arm yourself, too, with patience and sacrifice your
sufferings to this unhappy Greece and to Byron's glory. . . .' But
in the meantime, Byron himself was writing:

I watched thee when the fever glazed thine eyes,
    Yielding my couch and stretched me on the ground,
When overworn with watching, ne'er to rise
    From thence if thou an early grave hadst found. . .

Thus much and more; and yet thou lov'st me not,
    And never wilt! Love dwells not in our will.
Nor can I blame thee, though it be my lot
    To strongly, wrongly, vainly love thee still.

These lines are part of the last poem he ever wrote, and it was
not to Teresa that they were addressed, but to the unyielding
Loukas. Strange that he still had time and energy to give to love,
and suffering to spare for his private anguish. Yet it was an
external crisis that now took his attention: the nephew of
Karaiskakis, a Greek chieftain, had been wounded in a quarrel
with fishermen from Missolonghi and the uncle had, in retaliation,
seized a couple of hostages and the harbour-mouth fortress of
Vasiladi. At the same time and, as it proved, by collusion, the
Turkish fleet appeared off the coast. Sick as he was, Byron rode
out to show himself, demonstrate his confidence in the little
town's hastily manned defences and so combat the gathering
hysteria and terror of its people. And this time the tide turned;
the Turkish fleet withdrew and Karaiskakis, unsupported, tried
to flee as Suliote leaders marched to relieve Missolonghi, but was
soon captured. On Byron, however, the effect was disturbing;
Millingen recorded that his 'volcanic mind . . . was thrown by
these events into a violent state of commotion'. And still no real
successes existed to sustain him: Lepanto remained Turkish, the
Greeks remained disunited, Salona could still not be reached, and
promised little when it could. His own force was dispersed, the
money spent on it wasted. Loukas was adamant, Teresa far away
and, one suspects, increasingly unreal.

On 9 April, although his health was giving increased concern to
those about him, he went out riding for the first time in days. He
returned wet through. Pietro records, 'Two hours after his
return, he was seized with shuddering: he complained of fever

208

and rheumatic pains.' In the evening he was 'restless and melancholy. He said to me, "I suffer a great deal of pain. I do not care for death; but these agonies I cannot bear".' Despite a feverish night, he went riding again on the 10th; when Millingen visited him that evening, Byron quoted a gypsy prophecy made when he was a boy: 'Beware of your 37th year, my young Lord: beware!'

He was in pain that night – 'cold shuddering fits followed by burning intervals and wandering pains all over his body', as he reported to Bruno – but refused to be bled. Parry, the artilleryman, wanted to send him to the island of Zante, but an enormous and constantly increasing storm made this impossible. He rallied the following day; afraid, as he told Pietro, that he was losing his memory, he repeated Latin verses learned at school: 'I remembered them all except the last word of one of the hexameters.' And again he resisted his doctors' demand that they should bleed him.

The next day, 15 April, the sirocco still blew at gale force, imprisoning Byron on this flat and unforgiving coast. The doctors again pleaded to be allowed to do their worst, but Bruno had to record, 'Every argument that I or Dr Millingen put to him could not move him from his aversion. . . . My Lord replied, "I do not like it – I do not like it – you must have understood by now that neither your own prayers nor the chatter of other people will make me consent".' But when, in the evening, Parry came to visit him, Byron 'spoke of death . . . with great composure, and though he did not believe his end was so very near, there was something about him so serious and firm, so resigned and composed, so different from anything I had ever before seen in him, that my mind misgave me. . . .' Later, Byron said to him, 'My wife! My Ada! My country! The situation of this place, my removal impossible, and perhaps death, all combine to make me sad.'

He was ill that night, with violent spasms of coughing. Weakening, he promised to let the endlessly importunate doctors bleed him the following day. When Millingen reminded him of this in the morning and told him it was probably his only chance, he thrust his arm at the doctors with something of his old energetic irritation: 'Come; you are, I see, a damned set of butchers; take away as much blood as you will; but have done with it.' They took at least a pound of blood from him; 'the relief obtained did not correspond to the hopes we had entertained,' Millingen remarks primly. With the single-mindedness of true men of science, they therefore bled him a second time, hardly an hour after the first. Not surprisingly, he now slept for a while.

210

That night, however, he became feverish again and Tita took away the pistols and stiletto he always kept by him. On the 17th, he resisted at first when the doctors wanted to bleed him again, then gave in, but swiftly withdrew his permission. One feels that he was struggling against their mono-maniacal ministrations almost as fiercely as he was against death. When Pietro came to see Byron that evening he was appalled by his appearance which, he tells us, 'at once awakened the most dreadful suspicions'. Pietro had sprained his ankle; Byron told him to take care of his foot – 'I know by experience how painful it must be.'

'I am not afraid of dying,' he told Fletcher that evening. 'I am more fit to die than people think.' The old servant had helped him to get up, so that his bed could be made, but Dr Bruno pursued him into the sitting-room with further pleas to allow bleeding. Byron refused again, saying that 'if it is fated that I must perish from this disease, I shall die the same whether you have bled me or whether you leave me all my blood'. In this refusal he was confirmed by two other, more eminent, doctors who had been called in (though forbidden by Byron to comment); only Bruno, terrified by the prospect of inflammation of the brain, stood out. However, when he saw that the other three took a more cheerful view of Byron's condition, he too agreed that the bleeding should end, 'with all the more willingness since you with your opinion have given me good hopes. . . .'

On 18 April, however, Byron was once more delirious. Leeches were after all applied, and calmed him; but he was weaker now. He had, apparently, accepted the fact that he was dying. Outside his room the servants, alerted by the anxiety of the doctors, had begun to gather, hushed, some already weeping. Byron said to Millingen, 'Your efforts to preserve my life will be in vain. Die I must: I feel it. Its loss I do not lament; for to terminate my wearisome existence I came to Greece.' He added a request: 'Let not my body be hacked, or be sent to England. Here let my bones moulder. Lay me in the first corner without pomp or nonsense.' Millingen tells us 'with infinite regret' that during all this time Byron did not make 'any, even the smallest, mention of religion. At one moment I heard him say: "Shall I sue for mercy?" After a long pause he added: "Come, come, no weakness! Let's be a man to the last".'

Letters arrived from England. Hobhouse had written of Byron's finances – 'Your monied matters . . . are going swimmingly' – and of his reviving reputation in England – 'Your present endeavour

Giovanni Battista Falcieri
31 Maggio 1836

is certainly the most glorious ever undertaken by man.' Perhaps ten days before such news would have raised his spirits to the point where even disease might have been resisted; now, as Pietro Gamba noted, 'He had lost his senses; it was too late.' By mid-afternoon of that day, the Greek Easter Sunday, it was clear that his death was very close. Millingen and the two servants, Fletcher and Tita, were by his bed. 'The two first', Pietro recorded, 'could not contain their tears, and walked out of the room. Tita also wept, but he could not retire, as Byron had hold of his hand; but he turned away his face.' In a moment of lucidity, Byron called for Parry, but before he could arrive the fever had risen again.

And now it seems as if, briefly, without volition, Byron wore perhaps the last of his many masks, not now that of aloof aristocrat or unprincipled lecher, not that of hectic lover, dandy or melancholy poet, but that of the man of action, the warrior and hero, thus attempting for one more time to command reality, resetting the scene in the only way which could give meaning to his present condition: Parry, arriving, found him shouting, English and Italian alternating, 'Forward! Forward – courage – follow my example – don't be afraid. . . .' It was, for a moment, on the ramparts of Lepanto that he played the drama of the death that should have been.

Parry got Byron to take a little medicine and loosened the bandage around his head, which had been giving him pain; eased, he fell asleep and at that point Parry thought that 'he would wake no more'. But he did, sometimes to delirium, at others to clarity. When he raved, he mixed, as he had before, English and Italian. Around 5 pm he awoke apparently quite lucid and called Fletcher to him. There was an urgency in his manner; gasping for breath, he said, 'It is now nearly over, I must tell you all without losing a moment.' He would not let the old servant fetch pen and paper – 'Oh, my God! no, you will lose too much time' – but for all his determination, he could not remain coherent. He cried out, 'Oh, my poor dear child! My dear Ada! My God! could I but have seen her!', but then for a while could only murmur, his lips fluttering, the old servant straining to hear. Finally he said, 'Fletcher, now if you do not execute every order which I have given you, I will torment you hereafter if possible.' Fletcher had to tell him that he 'had not understood a word of what he said; to which he replied, "Oh, my God! then all is lost, for it is now too late!"' His despair was clear; but he could only speak in gasped, staccato bursts, a few words at a time: 'My wife! My child! My sister!'

OPPOSITE Tita, Byron's one-time gondolier and his faithful servant since his early days in Venice.

213

Soon he had fallen into even greater incoherence, murmuring disjointed series of names: 'Augusta. . . . Ada. . . . Kinnaird. . . . Hobhouse. . . .' In a sudden moment of clarity, however, he said, 'Why was I not aware of this sooner? Why did I not go home before I left for here?' At around six o'clock, he got up for the last time, to relieve himself. 'The damned doctors have drenched me so that I can scarcely stand,' he told those still waiting by the bed. He lay down again, soon murmured, 'I want to go to sleep now,' turned his back on these anxious observers and closed his eyes. At intervals now, he moaned faintly; blood from the leeches made livid streaks across his face. Thus watched helplessly by his friends, by the servants who had been closest to him, by the doctors, he lay in this condition for almost another twenty-four hours.

Perhaps, in one sense, it was weariness that killed him then, death the last and easiest escape from the reality of himself. The masks had failed him; the world, which he had been forced constantly to activate in order to receive back from it the certainty of his effective existence, had failed him – or must have seemed to him as though it had. He had gone to Greece to take up his last and most desired role, that of hero-general in the struggle for freedom; it was perhaps because he had always wanted to act that he had expressed such contempt for writing, action's substitute. But his opportunity was snatched away, his role after all outplayed – by the extras, the bit-players, the lesser stars. With the wished-for clarity of heroism thus occluded, everything seems to have become dull for him, cluttered, meaningless. The drama had turned into a farce, the 'travestie' he had feared. The final redemption of his limp, and of his masculinity, the overwhelming assertion of his best intentions, were denied to him.

So he lay through that long day, the weather still vicious over the Gulf of Patras. He should perhaps have realised long before that he had already gone beyond action, having become a legend: 'the greatest genius of the century', Goethe, who perhaps really was, had called him. For he had embodied a new self-awareness, had asserted in his words and his adventures that rebellious individualism which was to become for a hundred years the very essence of European civilisation. For twenty years and more, the mode of life of Europe's most vigorous and gifted young men was to be influenced, perhaps dominated, by what they understood of Byron.

They simplified him in order to understand him, smoothing Byron into 'the Byronic'. They did not penetrate, having no need

214

to, the paradoxes which gave him his intensity; the intensity was
enough for them. They understood his melancholy, his existential
despair, and the consequent cynicism with which he could regard
lesser or more affirmative emotions; they did not understand the
puritanism which fuelled his excesses. They understood his
aristocratic rebellion, his aloofness and disdain; they did not
understand his aristocratic conventionality, his instinctive calcu-
lation of the limits of outrage permitted a man of his class. They
understood his passion for the heroic; they did not understand the
passionate motivation given him by his crippled foot.

For they could know nothing, these 'Byronic' young men with
their wild hair, their sombre eyes, their flowing collars, of what
had really made Byron: his strange, doom-laden heredity, the
early deprivations, the perverse polarity within May Gray, trans-
mitted to him with all its distorting tension; and then the foot,
that foot, the uncontrollable, unalterable wound mocking his
every effort to dominate life, society and time; yet which,
ferociously, he overcame, fornicating it into oblivion, speaking it
out of sight, swimming it invisible. That foot, the existence of
which gave a sense of desperation to everything he did, which all
his actions sought to cancel out – and yet which would not go

217

The death of Byron saw the birth of the Byronic legend and effigies of the poet such as this Staffordshire figure were in great demand both in Britain and elsewhere in Europe.

away. And they could not suspect, as we might, his underlying lack of feeling, compensated for, too, by the forced ferocity of what he called love, his general greed for 'an attachment' which preceded all his particular relationships with women. Yet loving after all, almost despite himself, boys; and that too a wound, his masculinity made suspect – as it was, perhaps, by the very beauty which so overwhelmed the world.

Crippled within and without, classical in his reactions to an overpowering mother and an absent father, how with such handicaps, such beginnings, could he ever have become whole? Yet in the end, perhaps, he nearly did, the route difficult and perverse – trial, betrayal, failure, courage, sensitivity, corruption. Finally, achieving himself, he talks to us across a century and a half like none of his contemporaries, expressing in his letters and in *Don Juan* a wit, a relaxation, a tolerance which we need make no mental adjustments to understand. His verbal dexterity astounds us still, but not as much perhaps as his modernity. Of all those living then, only William Blake in his very different way speaks to us as clearly. Byron, in struggling for his personal freedom, presaged our own.

At around six o'clock in the evening of Monday, 19 April 1824, a storm shattered the dark skies above Missolonghi, lightning reflected dully in the black, surrounding waters; Parry called it 'one of the most awful thunder storms I ever witnessed'. Inside the sick-room, Fletcher watched the dying Byron: 'I saw my master open his eyes and then shut them, but without showing any symptoms of pain, or moving hand or foot. "Oh, my God!" I exclaimed, "I fear his lordship is gone". The doctors then felt his pulse, and said, "You are right – he is gone".'

The church at Hucknall Torkard where Byron is buried.
Seek out – less often sought
than found –
A soldier's grave, for
thee the best;
Then look around, and choose
thy ground,
And take thy rest.

Further Reading

WORKS OF BYRON

Rowland E. Prothero (ed.), *The Works of Lord Byron*, 6 vols, 1898-1901.

Peter Quennell (ed.), *Byron, A Self-Portrait. Letters and Diaries, 1798-1824.*

BIOGRAPHIES AND MEMOIRS

Lord Broughton (John Cam Hobhouse), *Recollections of a Long Life*, 6 vols, 1909-11.

C.L. Cline, *Byron, Shelley and their Pisan Circle*, 1952.

Sir John C. Fox, *The Byron Mystery*, 1924.

Count Pietro Gamba, *A Narrative of Lord Byron's Last Journey to Greece*, 1825.

Countess Teresa Guiccioli, *My Recollections of Lord Byron*, 1869.

Leigh Hunt, *Lord Byron and Some of His Contemporaries*, 1828.

Lady Caroline Lamb, *Glenarvon*, 3 vols, 1816.

Leslie A. Marchand, *Byron, A Portrait*, 3 vols, 1957 (also in one vol., 1970).

André Maurois, *Byron*, 1930.

Thomas Moore, *The Life, Letters and Journal of Lord Byron*, 1892.

Iris Origo, *The Last Attachment*, 1949.

William Parry, *The Last Days of Lord Byron*, 1825.

George Paston and Peter Quennell, *'To Lord Byron', Feminine Portraits Based upon Unpublished Letters, 1807-24*, 1939.

Mary Shelley, *The Letters of Mary Shelley*, 1944.
Mary Shelley's Journal, 1947.

Samuel Smiles, *A Publisher and His Friends: Memoir and Correspondence of the Late John Murray*, 2 vols, 1891.

Harriet Beecher Stowe, *Lady Byron Vindicated, A History of the Byron Controversy*, 1870.

J.D. Symon, *Byron in Perspective*, 1925.

Edward John Trelawny, *Recollections of the Last Days of Shelley and Byron*, 1858.
Records of Shelley, Byron and the Author, 1887.

Chronology

1788   *22 January* Birth of Byron at 16 Holles Street, London.

1791   *2 August* Death, at Valenciennes, France, of Byron's father, Captain John Byron.

1793   Byron starts at his first school, in Broad Street, Aberdeen.

1794-5 Byron attends Aberdeen Grammar School.

1798   *21 May* Byron becomes Baron Byron of Rochdale.

1801-5 Byron attends Harrow School. In 1803 he goes through a brief period of attachment to his neighbour, Mary Chaworth.

1806   *November* Publication of Byron's first collection of verse, *Fugitive Pieces*.

1807   *January* Publication of *Poems on Various Occasions* and *Hours of Idleness*. *March* Publication of *Poems Original and Translated*. *13 March* Byron takes his seat at the House of Lords.

1809   *March* Publication of *English Bards and Scotch Reviewers*. *2 July* Byron and Hobhouse sail from Falmouth for Greece and Turkey. They visit, among other places, Lisbon, Gibraltar, Malta, Jannina and Athens.

1810   Byron visits Greece and Turkey. *3 May* He swims across the Hellespont, from Sestos to Abydos.

1811   *14 July* Byron returns to England. *Late July* Death of Byron's mother.

1812   *10 March* Publication of the first two cantos of *Childe Harold*. First meeting with Lady Caroline Lamb. *25 March* First meeting with Annabella Milbanke. Affair with Lady Caroline Lamb. Affair with Lady Oxford.

1813   *June* Publication of *The Giaour*. *December* Publication of *The Bride of Abydos*.

1814   *January* Publication of *The Corsair*. *August* Publication of *Lara*. *9 September* Byron proposes marriage to Annabella Milbanke.

1815   *2 January* Marriage of Byron to Annabella Milbanke. *April* Publication of *Hebrew Melodies*. *10 December* Birth of Byron's daughter, Ada.

1816   *15 January* Separation of Byron and his wife. *February* Publication of *The Siege of Corinth* and *Parisina*. *21 April* Signature of the separation deed. *24 April* Byron leaves England for ever. *24 May* Arrival at Geneva. *26 May* First meeting with the Shelleys. Affair with Claire Clairmont. *5 October* Byron leaves Switzerland for Italy and settles in Venice. *18 November* Publication of the third canto of *Childe Harold*. *5 December* Publication of *The Prisoner of Chillon and other poems*. Affair with Marianna Segati.

1817   *12 January* Birth of Byron's daughter with Claire Clairmont,

Allegra. *29 April* Byron visits Rome with Hobhouse. *14 June* Byron moves to La Mira. *16 June* Publication of *Manfred*. Affair with Margarita Cogni. *December* Sale of Newstead Abbey.

1818   *22 February* Publication of *Beppo*. *28 April* Publication of the fourth canto of *Childe Harold*. *May* Byron moves into the Palazzo Mocenigo in Venice. *2 May* Allegra arrives in Venice.

1819   Byron meets and has an affair with Countess Teresa Guiccioli. *10 June* Byron moves to Ravenna. *28 June* Publication of *Mazzeppa* and the *Ode on Venice*. *15 July* Publication of the first two cantos of *Don Juan*. Byron moves to La Mira, then back to Venice.

1820   *6 July* Official separation of Teresa Guiccioli and her husband.

1821   *November* Byron moves to Pisa. *December* Publication of the third and fourth cantos of *Don Juan*, *The Two Foscari*, *Cain* and *Sardanapalus*.

1822   *January* First meeting with Trelawny. *20 April* Death of Allegra. *8 July* Drowning of Shelley and Williams. *16 August* Burning of Shelley's corpse on the beach at Viareggio. *September* Byron moves to Genoa. *15 October* Publication (in *The Liberal*) of *Vision of Judgment*. *22 November* Publication of *Werner*.

1823   *15 July* Byron sails for Greece.

1824   *January* Byron settles at Missolonghi. *9 April* Byron, whose health has been poor for some time, catches a chill in the rain. *19 April* Death of Byron at Missolonghi. *16 July* Byron's remains are buried in Hucknall Torkard, near Nottingham.

List of Illustrations

226

Several extracts in this book are reproduced by kind permission of John Murray, controller of Byron copyrights, and excerpts from diverse letters from Lord Byron by kind permission of Lord Lytton.

Index